Beyond Bliss

A Journey to the Ultimate Truth

A Short Biography of
Sri Shivarudra Balayogi Maharaj

Dr Bruce Young

Beyond Bliss

A Journey to the Ultimate Truth

A Short Biography of Sri Shivarudra Balayogi Maharaj

ISBN 0-9758478-0-5

National Library of Australia Cataloguing-in-Publication Data

Young, Bruce M.

Beyond bliss : a journey to the ultimate truth : a short biography of Sri Shivarudra Balayogi Maharaj.

ISBN 0-9758478-0-5

1. Sri Shivarudra Balayogi Maharaj. 2. Yogis - India - Biography. 1. Title.

294.5902

Published by :
Bruce M.Young
3 Hermite Rise, Sorrento, W.A. 6020
Australia

Printed by :
Neeraj Goel,
Delhi, India

His Divinity Sri Sri Sri Shivabalayogi Maharaj
(Swamiji)

His Holiness Sri Shivarudra Balayogi Maharaj
(Baba)

Dedication

Offering this at the golden Lotus Feet of the Divine Guru,
dearest Baba,
Sri Shivarudra Balayogi Maharaj,
I pray that my tears of joy at finding Him may wash away the illusions of mind and ego, that I may become the tiniest dust of His Feet.

Introduction

Any biography can only ever give a tiny view of a life, a mere aspect or two of a multi-faceted gem, a slight glimpse through a window into the interior of a house. That is even more so in such an astonishing life as has been lived by Baba - a biography of such an extraordinary life and personality can give only a tiny glimpse through a window of a vast gilded palace.

I first met Baba almost against my will, fulfilling a family obligation as he had been invited to the house of my relatives and I really only went out of duty. As He entered the room however, He appeared so strikingly beautiful and regal as to take away one's breath - His handsome face, His golden complexion and His beautiful matted hair cascading over His broad, strong shoulders. Yet I remember it was oddly His Feet which drew my attention; He seemed to walk in a very measured, calculated manner as though planning each step in detail - more like a child. He took His place on the dais and commenced His brief talk. His shining eyes were like dark pools of the night sky leading to Infinity and one felt if they could simply dive into there, all worries would simply disappear. His golden voice - gentle, yet strong and sure - was entrancing, and instantly transported one to a place of peace and shelter. He spoke of the Self and the mind, and how the mind had come out of the Self and needed to go back there - that only then would one find true Peace. His voice carried a calm assuredness and his words an all-embracing, all-encompassing wisdom which answered every question I had ever had. He then initiated those present into the technique of *dhyana* meditation and after we had practiced this together as a group, I remember at the end of the program sitting dumb-found on the floor unable to move or react. The only thought which came was, "This is IT!"

So it was through the desire to give a glimpse of this enormous personality and exceptional life and to give assurance to those who read it that miracles of achievement still do occur on this Earth, that this biography has come about. While it records events of His life, it does not pretend to be an exhaustive, complete register of these. Rather it is an assembly of events - some as focal points of this life, some instructive of His philosophy and teachings, and all as accurate to the events as I have been able to achieve. If there are errors in the script they are the author's, rather than the subject's.

The title itself, 'Beyond Bliss', was chosen to portray one extraordinary aspect of His life and teachings – the experience of the real Self is indescribable, so indefinable that it is beyond the Supreme Bliss so often referred to in so many texts as the aim of all spiritual efforts.

Baba Himself has been very generous in guiding in the compilation of the story, both with His time and His encouragement.

My small contribution to this work is only one of several. Others initially assembled the information about Baba's early life and in particular Rekha Sharma, and Carol and Charles Hopkins did most of this work. For the chapter on Swamiji's life I have made extensive use of the text written by His senior disciple General Hanut Singhji. My wife Anusuya has, as always, been my great supporter and has put in many hours reviewing the wording, and Baba's aide Rahul Ghosh has assisted with a different point-of-view where required.

Some Indian words have been used in the text where there is no true English equivalent. I have tried to keep this to a minimum, and to assist the reader a short glossary has been provided to assist in understanding non-English terms used.

May the Divine Guru bless that this simple text may give readers a thirst to know more of Him and to be in His Divine Presence, and thus be guided to their true home in the Self.

1st November 2005 **– Bruce Young**

Foreword

During the brief history of human habitation on this planet, there is a rare and extraordinary phenomena worthy of careful study, each and every time it occurs. The phenomena of which I speak is the appearance of a true Yogi. This is when God energy manifests in physical form and walks among us as a fellow human. And although God manifests in all of us, only a Yogi is continually aware of this and lives every moment fully immersed in God consciousness. Undoubtedly there are many Yogis who are spared fame and become known only to the few who are near them. Others have more outward or worldly missions and become widely known.

This book is the story of one such Yogic phenomenon. It documents the story of Sri Shivarudra Balayogi from before birth until present times. It is the story of exceptional God consciousness evolving into continuous manifestation in the body of an exceptionally pure soul. As you will learn, this manifestation did not happen spontaneously. It was an unfolding carried out over many years under the guidance of the great master Shivabalayogi Maharaj. This is a story of extreme, unswerving devotion and faith that can seem nearly incomprehensible to most of us. After years of intense discipline, hard physical and mental work, coupled with selfless service to humanity, Sri Shivarudra Balayogi underwent the final great test of tapas. Following this five year period of seclusion, intense spiritual practice and continual meditation, Sri Shivarudra Balayogi returned to his life mission of humble service to humanity. He freely gifts his love and knowledge to all who wish to receive it. So long as his earthly body holds out, he will continue with his mission of teaching meditation, encouraging spiritual practice, initiating God consciousness, and easing of human suffering.

Such love and commitment to God and fellow human is divinely inspired and easily sensed when in the presence of such a master. The transmittal of his energy is so complete as to make a permanent impact on those with the good fortune of seeking to meet him on either the spiritual or physical plane. Once this meeting has occurred, one has only to think of him to receive answers to spiritual questions or to gain further guidance on one's personal path towards God consciousness.

This book chronicles the life of an emerging Yogi. The news of the world is so often filled with stories of chaos, strife, sadness and human failure. However, the story of Sri Shivarudra Balayogi is a rare and welcome story of hope and inspiration for humankind. The greatness of God lies within all of us, but it is the rare soul who inspires us to reach within and to live that greatness. Sri Shivarudra Balayogi is one such soul, who manifests the power to change lives, inspire God consciousness and create peace.

Portland, Oregon
November, 2005

– Dr. Steve Scheer

Index

List of Photos

1

Advent and Ancestry

It began quietly and without fanfare in a small town in south India, when the local doctor's wife delivered a beautiful baby boy. No one there realized the immense significance of what had taken place - that one of the Great Ones had taken human form to bless and guide a lost and suffering humanity to their true home.

Srinivasa Dikshitar was born on 20th September, 1954 as the youngest child of Shankara and Sharada Dikshitar in the small town of Kolar in Karnataka state in the south of India. The family belonged to the Brahmin caste whose historic role was to carry on the priestly duties and study of scriptures for the Indian society - of the societies of this world, that eldest sister which values the pursuit of spiritual truth above all other human activity.

Shankara's family was very pious and for generations had carried on their scholarly and priestly duties with great care and devotion. His family had moved many generations before from the pilgrimage town of Kancheepuram in Tamil Nadu state to the Kolar District of the state of Karnataka.

One remarkable forebear was Shamanna who was born to his priest father Kashipatayya in 1819. Educated in the *Vedas* (the Hindu scriptures) as a child, he dreamt of becoming a monk but - perhaps out of respect for his parent's wishes - married and continued his worldly duties with detachment and devotion. At the age of 29, he experienced a dazzling vision in which a glowing divine being appeared and directed him to perform a fire ceremony called '*Agnishta Homam*' which is performed for nine days, to propitiate Lord Shiva[1] for peace and liberation from worldly existence. He later described this astounding experience to his father who though believing firmly in the verity of Shamanna's vision, felt it would be beyond their financial capacity to carry out such a large undertaking. Somehow the king of Mysore eventually came to hear of the vision and after interviewing the young priest, offered to finance the *homam* which was then carried out successfully along with all it's accompanying mass-feeding and gifts for the poor and needy, and the attendant saints and learned scholars.

About a year later Shamanna had a second amazing dream-vision in which Lord Shiva instructed him to perform '*Poundarika Homam*' ; when in the dream he asked Lord Shiva how the financial burden would be met, the dream abruptly ended. He spent the following day wondering and puzzled, and enquiring into the details of how such an *homam* was performed, finding that it is carried out continually over forty days and accompanied by austerities such as taking only a single glass of milk once a day as nourishment and the necessary attendant mass feeding and charity. Knowing such a vast undertaking to be beyond his finances but with deep faith that Lord Shiva had ordained it and therefore would guide him to successfully complete the task, he was directed the next night in another dream to approach a merchant in the next village for financial support. Though the merchant was well known to be miserly, with faith in the Lord's direction, Shamanna approached the merchant only to find that the merchant himself had also had a dream of Lord Shiva in which he was instructed to help the pious Brahmin. Though previously skeptical of the dream's portent, when Shamanna then approached him the merchant was surprised to see the dream coming into reality and experienced a great change

---

[1] *Lord Shiva* - Lord Shiva is one of the Trinities of the concept of God in Hinduism. See Glossary.

of heart, agreeing to finance the *homam* and all it's needs.

The *Poundarika Homam* was thus performed by Shamanna and his pious wife over forty-one days with saints, scholars and devotees in their thousands coming to participate. The daily mass feedings and gifts to the participants and the needy were thus enormous. Following the successful completion of this vast endeavour Shamanna became widely known as 'Eshwara Poundarika Dikshitar' and was held in high regard by all. In his older age he renounced the world and retired to the pilgrimage town of Kashi (Benares) where he spent his remaining days in meditation and service to the poor and needy.

His descendants lived a simple priestly life of devotion and service and his great grandson similarly undertook several great *homams*, coming to be known as 'Yagna Narayana Dikshitar'. After the birth of his son Shankara Dikshitar, when the child was only six months old , he unfortunately passed on from this world and Shankara's mother in turn only lived another five years after this. As greedy relatives subsequently took all the property acquired by his family, the young boy was left penniless, with only God to call on as his mother and father.

Srinivasa's mother, Sharada was similarly born into a devout Brahmin family and her birth was blessed by the saint, Sri Shankaracharya of Koodalimutt. This happened when the saint visited her parents' home when Sharada's mother was still expectant with the child. After being received with all due honours, the venerable sage was pleased with their care and devotion and invited the husband, Narayana Iyer, to accompany him on his journey to the next town. While this was a rare privilege and great blessing, the Brahmin was perplexed, knowing his wife was due to deliver the baby soon. He explained the situation in which he found himself to the Shankaracharya, "Oh Reverend Saint, may I be forgiven for not accompanying you because my wife is expected to deliver a child any moment and she needs me by her side."

Broadly smiling, the sage replied, "Do not worry about the

delivery. A female child will be born - name her 'Sharada'. She will be a noble, pious lady and will bear noble children in her womb."

'Sharada' is the name of the presiding deity of the temples at Koodali and also nearby Sringeri. The deity was installed by the great philosopher-yogi Adi Shankaracharya[2], as an embodiment of Saraswati (goddess of divine knowledge) many centuries before and it was at Koodali that he had established a monastery of which this present Shankaracharya was the head.

With great faith and devotion Narayana Iyer accompanied the Shankaracharaya as suggested and when he returned, discovered that the couple had been blessed with a beautiful baby daughter.

These two blessed souls, Shankara and Sharada, were married in 1926. Shankara Dikshitar, having lost both his parents in his early childhood and thus growing up in difficult circumstances, had developed an iron will and with deep faith and devotion to God had carried on through hard work and perseverance. He worked at the home of relatives to earn fees for his studies. He learnt a harsh lesson of the world when as a young boy he walked about 20 kilometres to the house of a close relative to request some money for school fees, only to be refused and ridiculed by the drunken relation. This galvanized his strong will and he learnt through efforts, determination and will power to endure through hardship and succeed. Through his determined efforts, though his circumstances made it an enormous task, he eventually graduated as a doctor with the aim of helping the needy.

Looking for a wife, he was blessed to find Sharada who also demonstrated great integrity and nobility of character. Shankara's religious observance was predominantly his work as a doctor, which he performed as a service to God and humanity - though he did

---

[2] *Adi Shankaracharya* - (also Adi Shankara). Great Yogi-teacher of India who spread the teachings of 'non-dualism'. See Glossary.

perform morning devotional prayers to Lord Venkateshwara[3], praying and offering flowers. In contrast Sharada's religious observance was more orthodox in that she regularly attended the temples, praying and performing the various rituals traditional in Indian society.

After graduating from medical college in 1932, still penniless, Shankara formed a desire to work in Burma (which he had visited with a relative in 1924) and to raise the money for the journey, Sharada selflessly offered to sell the jewellery she had been given as a dowry. He travelled to Burma where she joined him a year later, and there started work as a doctor. Sharada supported him in his aim of service to the poor and needy, and they would even sometimes purchase food and supplies for their patients. This meant that he kept just enough for his family's basic requirements, using the rest of his income to serve those in need, and thus the couple sometimes lived in straitened circumstances.

In 1939 Sharada gave birth to a daughter, but her husband was away at the time on his charity work and when the child became ill the young mother could not find adequate medical care to help the infant, and thus the daughter passed away. Two years later they had a son who they named Vijay Kumar and then later she delivered twins. Shankara was again away for some weeks on charitable work when the twins were born and when the male baby of the pair developed a fever it proved too much for his tiny body and he died, leaving only his twin sister who they named Vijaya Lakshmi. The World War had overtaken Burma during this time and during the Japanese occupation Shankara worked under the Japanese invaders but still found time, three days a week, to continue his humanitarian work amongst the less fortunate. He treated his Japanese patients as well as he did his other charges - for him, he was a doctor and they were patients, regardless of their outer garb. He used to say, "I have always thought it shouldn't

---

[3] *Lord Venkateshwara* - An Incarnation of Lord Vishnu whose temple at Tirupati is famous all over India.

make any difference to me, as to which place or country the patient belongs. No matter to which religion, caste or race the patient belongs, a patient is a patient to me - injured, physically suffering, mentally tortured and in need of a doctor's attention - that is all I know."

Due to her deep devotion to God, Sharada never felt any fear at all - she simply used to keep singing the glory of God whether she was working with her husband or at home alone. Once during the wartime when her husband was posted in a place called Tounjee his piles problem had become acute, but owing to his preoccupation with the charity work which he often undertook, he had ignored his own ailment for too long. Finally some friends insisted that he undergo an operation. As the town had become very unsafe, he wanted to send Sharada and the children to a more secure place. Usually she would never argue with her husband, but that day Sharada was feeling very strange, and perhaps perceived by a divine intuition that some danger may befall her husband. She became unusually adamant and would not agree to go away alone and insisted that he also come with her. Shankara was surprised at this, as before this his wife had never argued with him or forced him to do anything against his will, so he took extra note of her unusual insistence. Finally he managed to get ten days' leave and left Tounjee with the family. Now because of the war, the train system in Burma was in chaos - there were no proper railway stations, no one to manage any stations, and nobody knew which train was moving where. Sometimes people would have to wait for two or three days inside the train before it would start moving. There was an ever-present danger of bombing raids and nobody was sure of living to see the next moment. Chaos and suffering were universal.

In these extreme circumstances, all they could do was wait for a train to come by chance, and they were left indeed to wait for two days with a few clothes and only some biscuits as food, before a train finally came. Even after finally boarding the train, it took another two days before it eventually moved out. Shankara at first thought that he would leave his wife at a safer place in Rangoon and then return to his duty, but when they finally reached Rangoon they heard over the radio that the railway line on which they had just travelled as well as the town of Tounjee where they had been living, had been bombed heavily the day after they left, and for the most part destroyed and most of the residents killed. Some unknown Superior Power had thus guided the small family to safety.

They thus endured great danger and hardship throughout the war and even when the war was over, it left Burma's economy in tatters. In 1949 Sharada developed a strong desire to return to her motherland India for the children's education - perhaps it was a divine inspiration. Discussing the return with her husband, he replied that he still felt destined to work among the poor of Burma, but recognizing her selfless desire for the children's welfare he sent the rest of the family back to India, though he stayed on in Burma to work. However in the year that followed he subsequently found that with his wife and family away he became very lonely and his health - already not strong because of his neglect of his own body's needs in the anxious service of the poor - deteriorated considerably. Thus in August 1950 he finally resigned his position in Burma and returned to India to join his wife and two children. Returning to Kolar to live, the family was soon blessed with another son who they named Satyanarayana.

The doctor continued his charitable work here, and he again commonly provided free medical care to the poor in the area. He was straightforward in his speech and dealings with all, and abhorred injustice or deceit in any form, and this meant he came to be widely respected in the district. He was not money-minded, but believed in work. He told his children that if money gets accumulated, it attracts people who will be tempted to misuse it. He had experienced this in his own life, with the relatives who took away the family wealth by devious means and were then so ungenerous to others. He had thus decided that in his life he would not make money to accumulate property and wealth, but work for the benefit of humanity. He would instruct his children that Character, Education, Sincerity and Charitable Temperament were the property he would like to give them. He considered Determination and Character to be his constant companions.

Just as Shankara was admired for his work and strength of character by all in the district, his wife was also held in similar high esteem. Sharada worked equally hard, attending to her husband and his patients and to the young children that God had entrusted to her, and was always kind to others. She never gossiped or criticized people, and worked ceaselessly, absorbed in singing *bhajans* (devotional songs) or reading about God. If poor relatives from nearby villages came to the town for work, for medical attention and so on, they would freely visit the home and were never sent away without being fed. She always prayed to God not to make her bedridden and to let her be helpful to others. Though deeply religious and observant in that, her wisdom, like her husband's, was practical and one of her favourite pieces of advice was that, "If one can't help someone, then at least one should not bother them." Though pure at heart she was nevertheless very worldly-wise.

Whenever beggars came to the house she always found something to give them, advising her children, "You never know - God may come in any form to test your character and purity of mind. You cannot fool God." She was never rude to anybody, and the couple never dwelt on the difficulties they had experienced in their life. They always said to their children, "Education is the property we give you and remember Character shall be your wealth. Develop and cultivate these and nobody can rob you."

Thus this saintly couple brought up their young brood carefully and lovingly. Shankara did not believe in corporal punishment and was quite liberal in his upbringing of his children, but he did impart a foundation of good advice for living well and happily, in particular the application of one's mind to a given goal and the virtue of sincerity in one's dealings with others. His wife, along with her strong sense of devotion to God, possessed in herself - and also nurtured in her children - enormous inner strength and an iron will, though it was tempered by a mother's wisdom and love.

So it was to this saintly couple, shining examples of devotion, iron willpower and selfless service, that Srinivasa was born.

2

His Early Years

Srinivasa, affectionately called 'Seenu' by his family, grew up in this safe and loving environment and being the youngest in the family was naturally cosseted by all. A handsome child, all who saw him formed an attachment to him easily - even as a baby, the adorable child possessed such charm that many a time, simply out of fascination, neighbours would quietly take him away to their homes to feed him - leaving his family searching for him from house to house.

He had a happy childhood surrounded by the care and guidance of his parents and lived the life of a normal youngster in India. He possessed a particular gift for mimicry, especially of musical instruments, and it was common for the neighbours on hearing the 'concerts' he would thus perform in his room, to enquire of the family who it was that was learning such a variety of musical instruments. He similarly showed a great skill with languages and loved acting. While still young he would perform the whole story of the Ramayana, acting out all the many parts in the epic himself, though his favourite was that of Rama's hero-disciple Hanuman. However he performed his academic studies only from a sense of duty, having no great interest in the seemingly dry and uninteresting subjects, but even with this lack of interest his innate high intelligence enabled him to perform well, though he did not excel. He enjoyed playing the usual childhood games and sports but was not overly concerned at winning. In a sign of the great soul that lay hidden within, he showed an uncommon selflessness and awareness of what would make others feel content. For example he didn't mind being teased if he lost, if it made others happy when they won.

The young boy was influenced and inspired by his mother who was devoted to God and it was she who helped him understand the need to apply the mind, and the principle that it is through the mind that one can reach God. As with most Hindu mothers, she recounted devotional stories to him from the Ramayana, the Mahabharata and the Bhagavatam and these great spiritual epics were Seenu's bedtime stories. His father, being more 'practically' orientated, instructed him to use his mental abilities with focus - directing him for instance if reciting prayers to not just simply recite the words aimlessly, but to focus on the words with his full attention. These teachings imparted when he was so young and in his formative years, had a strong impact in forming his future attitudes in life.

However even though his childhood was a happy one, from the young age of five or six years he started to experience a vague feeling that there was something missing in his life. This was an acute spiritual hunger which Seenu experienced as a pain in the stomach - albeit one which was not truly physical. Along with this came a peculiar pain of not belonging, a strong sense of alienation from the world, which he later described as a feeling that in being in this world he had been transported into a strange new dimension which was not his true home.

The young boy's first obvious spiritual experience occurred when he was around six or seven years old and he overheard his sister singing '*Bhaja Govindam*', the song composed by Adi Shankaracharya centuries before. This song had a mesmerising effect on Seenu and the deep-thinking child immediately learnt the Sanskrit words and verses and started singing it himself. '*Bhaja Govindam*' is a famous scriptural song which emphasises the ultimate futility of worldly achievements and possessions. Watching her young son, Sharada one day warned him not to be too influenced by the scripture - she was concerned that because of the extraordinary level of renunciation and detachment it recommended, if one followed the song's teaching literally then one could not function normally in the world. She suggested he read other scriptures instead. This made the young boy all the more curious and so he set about learning in detail the meaning of every word of the text of the song. In the song, Adi Shankara reminds us that when death comes, no scholarly wisdom or material possession will help one's soul spiritually - only surrender to the Divine will guarantee one's salvation from the cycle of birth and death. The song exhorts a scholar to "sing the glory of God and adopt His consciousness into your mind, for when the end comes to the physical body, none of your worldly scholarship, wealth or possessions are going to come to your rescue." The song quickly obsessed Seenu with its dire warning to be detached from worldly things.

Around that time the young boy also became preoccupied with the thought of death. He had already been scared of death and if someone in the area died he would literally try to sleep the fear off and go into quietness. He used to wonder why a person should have to die at all and what the purpose of life was - if one simply had to die in the end. These profound spiritual questions simmered within the young Seenu and he kept himself absorbed in sublime thoughts of God and the mystery of birth and death. He would often ask himself whether people are born along with their physical body and if one actually ceases to exist at the time of death. He wondered why, if it was true that one is really the immortal soul as the scriptures declared, that one was not consciously aware of it.

And another question began to form in his mind - a simple question, but astute and profound in its implications: "If happiness exists, why is it that we don't havc it all the time? Why can't we be happy for all the 24 hours of the day, 7 days of the week?" This simple yet profound question became a focal point of his querying - along with the question of "Who am I ?" - and these questions formed the basis of the spiritual enquiry and endeavours into which he now launched. He began to feel these two themes of permanent happiness and true identity as inexorably linked, and pursued and examined these questions using his razor-sharp intellect - an intellect which possessed a remarkable ability to cut to the central core of an issue and extract the Truth buried deep within. This clear and sharp analytic ability enabled him to easily see to the heart of a matter under enquiry, quickly distinguishing the important elements of a question and its answer. This deeply incisive analysis of the essential elements of matters was an innate skill which continued to grow only stronger throughout his enquiries.

During his teenage years he spent his time visiting temples where he loved the serenity and solitude, quietly sitting in a corner, but found he avoided the holy shrines at busier times and during public festivals due to the noise and bustle. He found that sitting calmly in the temple precinct, his mind, which only rarely experienced any significant agitation, used to become more quiet and peaceful. He was devotional in temperament and had tremendous faith in God which was nurtured by his parents, and indeed the whole devout society around him.

Srinivasa was strongly attracted to the great saint Sai Baba of Shirdi[4], and had a deep-seated interest in the philosophy of Adi Shankaracharaya which had been initiated by the song '*Bhaja Govindam*'. Intent on grasping the inner meaning of these masters' teachings, he gradually absorbed the meaning of *jnana* (knowledge), *bhakti* (devotion) and *vairagya* (detachment) which he always considered as belonging together as different aspects of the one whole. He worshipped all forms of God and was equally likely to be found in a Shiva or Devi temple.

Nevertheless, the fundamental question which preoccupied him during this worship was the nature of 'That' which existed behind and beyond the manifested form of the temple stone

---

[4] *Sai Baba of Shirdi* - A famous Indian saint of the 19th and 20th centuries who had followers from both the Muslim and Hindu faiths.

idol which was worshipped as a symbol of God. Dwelling on these matters, he experienced periods of discomfort and restlessness, and the unusual thought kept coming to him that peace would come if he could find a way to 'switch off' the universe.

" *I often felt uncomfortable on seeing the world. I used to think how peaceful it would be if there was a technology which could switch off the universe.* "

A turning point was reached when he asked himself the fundamental question of whether the universe would come to an end if he put an end to his own body. Seenu's father had passed away suddenly in 1967, a few months before the boy's thirteenth birthday. This event didn't appear to have any effect on his mind at the time outside the normal grief that one would expect, and didn't cause any serious financial problems for the family as his older brother Vijay was able to take charge of looking after them. Nevertheless the thought of ending the life of the body kept repeatedly occurring to him during this time. Since violence was alien to his nature he resolved not to use violent means to put an end to his body, feeling that then in this way his mind would not thus become violent.

Following his father's death his brother had taken up a post in Madras and his mother went to live there with Vijay, while after completing the tenth grade exam Seenu entered the nearby college. He was aware that his father had kept a supply of sleeping tablets at his home and he quietly thought to himself, "without making the mind violent, I can end the life of this body".

So it was that on one night in November 1968, he took the container of sleeping pills to the room where he studied and prayed to God that when his body died, he would reach God Himself and not be reborn in this world or in any other world. With such elevated thoughts in his mind the young Seenu systematically swallowed a huge quantity of sleeping pills - some seventy or eighty - and half a dozen naphthalene balls, then lay down and went to sleep.

With his mother away in Madras he had been taking his meals at the nearby home of some relatives and they became concerned when he failed to appear for his regular meal at their home. When they came to the house to investigate, they were shocked to see him lying motionless on the bed. They tried to wake Seenu up by splashing water on him and shaking his body, but after they received no response to this, they finally called a doctor. After finding the pulse was very slow the doctor realized the seriousness of the young boy's condition and ordered that he be admitted to hospital immediately.

The drugs and toxins had made him unconscious and the hospital staff initially felt he was unlikely to live, but he was eventually revived after his stomach was pumped and was very fortunate to have survived, though it took several days for him to properly return to normal consciousness. While in hospital, Seenu told the doctor everything that had occurred, relating the events in detail - he told the astonished doctor that he had just wanted to reach God!

Naturally this all came as great shock to the family as no one had considered that such a thing could be brewing - they had never seen the slightest hint of any unhappiness or emotional disturbance in Seenu. His sister Vijaya Lakshmi rushed home from Mysore to be with him. When he was finally discharged from the hospital after about ten days, he was unable to explain to the family what was happening to him or why he had done this - being so young and grappling with such vast cosmic questions, he could not express his feelings adequately. When his elder brother and his mother asked, "Are you facing any problems? Are you unhappy? Do you have any desires?", Seenu replied honestly, "No, I am totally satisfied." All he could say was, "I don't want this world."

Such a study of these deep questions of life and death, and the meaning and purpose of existence are not often undertaken by one so young, and it was difficult for his family to understand that he was not depressed in the normal sense - simply searching earnestly for true answers to the real questions of life. Seenu's relatives thought it might have been the isolation and loneliness of being away from the family which had caused him to try to take his own life and they probably expected his attitude to change if he had more company and interaction with people. So in the next year they brought him to Mysore and he was enrolled in the college there, where he studied botany. In the college he shared a room with his older brother Satyanarayana and he was also able to visit his sister in Mysore as well. However these external changes did not make any difference to the inner development occurring within him, as events would soon reveal.

Seeking a way to God other than by ending his body's existence, he started to read more on spiritual subjects and was drawn to the teachings of Sri Ramakrishna Paramahamsa[5] and Adi Shankaracharya. From this he started to develop a clearer concept of the Self and he began to develop a strong desire for a true Guru to guide him. Though struck by the teachings of these great sages, he still wanted to know the practical techniques, the technology, by which the mind could go beyond the world to that Eternal, Absolute Truth of Existence. He later discovered the life-story and Self-enquiry philosophy of Sri Ramana Maharshi[6] and this further stimulated the desire in him to achieve the liberation these Great Souls had attained.

While for a few months it appeared he had returned to normal, it wasn't long before he started feeling uncomfortable and restless again because of his involvement with worldly life, minimal though it was compared to others. This restlessness was an affliction which troubled his otherwise peaceful state, even though there was no particular thing he could identify in the world around him which actually bothered him. It wasn't a desire to escape problems in the conventional sense, since his mind didn't focus on good

---

[5] *Sri Ramakrishna Paramahamsa* - A famous saint who lived in Bengal at the end of the19th Century.

[6] *Sri Ramana Maharshi* - A great Tamil saint of 20th Century who expounded the teaching of Self-enquiry.

Family : (from L to R) Shankara Dikshitar, Vijay Kumar, Satyanarayana, Srinivasa, Vijaya Lakshmi and Sharada Dikshitar

versus bad; it just longed for a more peaceful existence.

Around the age of fifteen, persistent thoughts of ending the life of his body started to return, even though he spent his time visiting temples and enjoying the solitude there in an effort to quieten this restless feeling. Around November he decided to make a bolder attempt to end his physical life. Once again he addressed God saying, "You are my God. I'm going to kill this body, but I must reach only you!" Thus saying, he took some kerosene, poured it all over his body, struck a match and set his shirt alight - it instantly exploded into flames.

Shocked by the sudden violence of the experience, which he had previously envisioned as being sacred, he abruptly tore off his blazing shirt in alarm. Luckily neither his hair nor his pants had caught alight. He stood trembling for about half an hour from the shock of the ordeal and jolted by the agitation it induced in his normally quiet mind, then sat down in front of a photo of Shirdi Sai Baba in whom he had developed such great faith. Gradually as his mind quietened, the thought emerged from within that perhaps he was not ready to die in such a violent way and that he shouldn't end his life in this manner. Thoughts also came that there was no guarantee that he would actually reach God this way and that in the Indian spiritual tradition there was another approach available - namely to live the life of a monk away from worldly things.

Srinivas sat down and wrote a letter to his brother in Madras explaining what had happened and saying that he didn't want to live in this world - that he wanted to go away and become a *sannyasin* (monk). In the letter he requested his brother's permission because of the great regard he had for him and also because his brother was now the head of the family. Without receiving his brother's and his mother's permission he felt he should not leave home. On receiving the message, Vijay rushed from Madras to Mysore to be with him and spoke to him at length, advising him to wait until he had found a proper Guru or some guidance. When his brother asked why he was experiencing these feelings, the only reply the young Seenu could give at the time was that the world was transitory and that there was no reason to live in it. It was difficult for the young boy to put his deep feelings of disquiet into clear words. He tried to illustrate his unease by pointing out the futility of the worldly existence - saying that if we stop eating we'll starve to death, but even if we continue to eat as much as we want we'll die eventually anyway! - so what is the point of living a worldly life?

After a long discussion Seenu finally agreed to his elder brother's suggestion to stay at home for the moment, knowing it would be too much of a shock for his mother if he was to leave home abruptly at his time. He agreed to wait until he found a Guru and also that he would only leave with his mother's permission. Reluctantly he continued his studies and the following year his mother also came to live with him in Mysore.

All through this time, he never participated much in any of the social gatherings of the family,

" *By nature I would not mingle with many people - I was happy within myself. I liked solitude and serenity.* "

However he was a regular visitor to the Hanuman temple which stood opposite the family home. Here Seenu spent most of his time quietly absorbed in thoughts of birth and death, and the existence of the Self. He struck up an acquaintance with a young *sannyasi* (monk) named Anandji who was also interested in genuine spiritual endeavours and was a priest in the Lakshminarayanam Swami temple which was situated behind the main Chamundeshwari temple on the Chamundi Hills outside Mysore. His new friend showed him an isolated cave in the Chamundi Hills, Nagara Theertha, where he could quietly meditate without being disturbed by the worldly noise and bustle of the city. Several times a week he would pack some *rotis* (flat bread) as though going to college and then secretly slip away to this isolated cave, spending the day there in the quiet, serene solitude in contemplation and meditation. Following the teachings of Ramana Maharshi he spent long hours daily in this isolated haven, in meditation observing where the sense of Self originated. Every evening he would also visit different temples around Mysore - on Monday it was the Shiva temple, Tuesdays the Hanuman temple, Wednesdays the temple of Kartikeya, Thursday the Shirdi Sai Baba temple, on Friday the famous temple in the Chamundi Hills where the presiding deity was Goddess Chamundishweri, Saturdays the temple of Lord Venkateshwara and Sundays the Chamundishweri temple once more.

" *Quietly I waited and I knew that soon my Guru would come and take me away. This knowing came from within.* "

3

A Strange Voice, then Love at First Sight

In this way Srinivas waited for God to reveal Himself in the form of Guru - he had tremendous faith that it would eventually occur if he was genuine in his desire and endeavours. Waiting thus for his Guru, most of his time in the mornings and evenings were spent in the temples of Mysore where he used to sit in a quiet corner and become absorbed in thoughts of Guru, birth, death and the Ultimate Truth. The other sadhana which the world did not notice was being conducted in the serenity of the Naagara Teertha cave's solitude in the forests of the Hills, where he would remain absorbed meditating on thoughts of the Self for long hours on end.

One evening during his contemplation, sitting quietly in the Hanuman temple near his home, Seenu suddenly heard a voice whispering in his ears, "Shivabalayogi is your Guru. It is He you are waiting for. You will get everything from Him." Opening his eyes and looking around, to his amazement there was absolutely no one in sight! - this was a quiet temple hardly frequented by people. But he could not forget the name Shivabalayogi; it was continually ringing in his ears.

For the next few days Seenu went on enquiring about Shivabalayogi from all the people he met in the temple, hoping to find more clues as to what the experience had meant. However nobody he spoke to could tell him anything about Shivabalayogi. Several days passed by without any fruitful information being uncovered, until one day when he was in the Mysore town centre.

While walking through one of the crowded streets, again all of a sudden he heard a voice whisper, "Go to Raghavendraswami[7] Temple. There you will know about your Guru." Thrilled, he turned around to see who it was that had spoken, but once more there was no one in sight!

Seenu wondered who it could be that had whispered this to him - could it be the same voice who had told him about the Guru when he was sitting in the temple precinct? Having only this whispered directive as a guide, he followed it and went immediately to the Raghavendraswami Temple.

"*I went to the temple. All along I could feel vibrations which gave me enormous peace and made the mind become quiet. Some thoughts were coming - not agitated, but peaceful thoughts. 'Whose is this voice? First it told me about Shivabalayogi, now it has told me the place where I would know about Shivabalayogi. Is this the Guru Himself choosing to convey the information in this way?'* "

When he reached the temple he found a priest was narrating a story from the scriptures to a small gathering of some elderly devotees. He joined the group to listen to the story but after some time he forgot his purpose in going there and became absorbed in the story of God. Suddenly he was brought back to consciousness of the world as the story-telling came to an end and the other people had dispersed. A man of about fifty years of age came to him, asking,

"What are you doing in the midst of these old people? " Seenu replied, "Is it wrong for young boys to listen to God's story?"

The man smiled, "I did not mean it like that. Normally.... people think that one should come to spiritual life only after finishing their worldly life and have reached old age. Yours is the age when one is supposed to be playing around and enjoying the world."

---

[7] *Raghavendraswami* - A seventeenth-century saint-poet of Karnataka in south India.

Spontaneously from the depth of his heart, the young boy replied, "I have become mentally old enough to go towards God. Perhaps many, many lives ago I was young. Now I am looking for my Guru."

Suddenly the man interrupted him, "Guru? I know a *Yogi*[8] who is my Guru and teaches meditation. Get initiated by Him and meditate - you will know God."

Naturally Seenu became curious and asked, "What is your Guru's name, Sir?"

"Shivabalayogi. Lord Shiva Himself initiated Him into twelve years of *tapas*[9]. Let's go to my home and I will give you a book describing His life and teachings. If you read this, you will know His greatness."

Seenu exclaimed, "Yes! I am looking for Shivabalayogi!"

" *We reached his home. I was lost in my own thoughts and was already at the Lotus Feet of my beloved Swamiji. The man told me that His devotees addressed Him as 'Swamiji', and gave me the book on Him and some other stories of God.*

I said, 'I can read the other stories later but I need to read about Swamiji immediately.'

Thus Swamiji came into my life or shall I say, I had come back into Swamiji's life.

My joy knew no bounds. I went on reading. My heart cried, 'I love You, Swamiji. I want You, Swamiji.' I didn't know what I meant. But my mind and heart were unanimous. I just wanted Swamiji.

Two days later when I went to return the book I was told by that person that Swamiji would be coming to Mysore to give darshan[10] *on the invitation of His devotees. At last the day was coming closer - the wait was coming to an end.*

---

[8] *Yogi* - One who has fulfilled the path of *Yoga* - has become one with the Divine Self.

[9] *Tapas* - A practice of spiritual austerity involving deep meditation for extended periods of many years. See Glossary.

Drowning in thoughts and feelings of 'Swamiji I love You. Oh! - my beloved Swamiji, I love You', I asked the gentleman, 'Where is He going to give His darshan*? Can you take me there, Sir?'*

'Yes. You can go with me. He will be giving darshan *at the foothills of the Chamundi Hills.'* "

It was Sri Shivabalayogi's custom every year after His birthday celebrations in His Bangalore ashram on 24th January to visit the Chamundi Hills before starting His mission tour for the year and so it was that on 5th February 1971, He came again to the hills. One of Swami Sivananda's disciples had invited Swamiji to visit the ashram there.

During the night just before this much-anticipated *darshan*, Seenu had a vivid dream-vision in which he found himself standing in the dark, in a queue. A person came to him, asking,

"Why are you standing in the queue? He is waiting for you. Come with me." In the dream Seenu followed the person quietly and entered a hall through a second door away from the queue. He beheld the glorious sight of Shivabalayogi sitting on the dais with crossed legs, dressed in a loin-cloth with His beautiful matted hair cascading over His shoulders. The *Yogi* smiled.

In his mind Seenu thought, "I have found Him."

Suddenly two figures appeared - one male and one female - and said, "This is your Guru and everything. Serve Him till the end."

Seenu wondered in the dream who they were and wanted to ask them, but as suddenly as they had appeared, they then disappeared.

The *Yogi* signalled to Srinivasa to come closer and with a warm smile and glow on His face, He asked, "What did they say? You know they were Shiva-Parvati (Lord Shiva and His consort

---

[10] *Darshan* - Darshan is a precious spiritual exercise for the devotee's eyes. To meet a *Yogi* is also darshan. See Glossary.

Goddess Parvati)."

" *My mind had become standstill; it was a spellbinding experience for me.*

Swamiji said, 'I know what They told you. They will make you do it. Now tell me - what do you want?'

Spontaneously it came out of my mouth, 'Give me Jnana *(Knowledge),* Bhakti *(Devotion) and* Vairagya *(Detachment).'*

He blessed me and then gave me a stick, saying, 'Keep this - you will get everything.'

I said, 'I want You, Swamiji.'

Then He took back the stick, broke it to pieces and threw it away, declaring, 'This could have given only worldly pleasures. If you want God, this stick is of no use.'

Then He poured vibhuti *(sacred ash) on my head, and whispered beautifully in a soft voice,*

' OM SHIVAYA SHIVABALAYOGENDRAYA
PARABRAHMANAYA '

and said, 'Keep repeating this name always. No harm can come to you and you will have the power to serve Me. Now you go.'

I came out. It was total darkness. Nobody was there - all those who were in the queue had gone or disappeared I suppose.

Suddenly a policeman appeared and asked, 'What are you doing here?'

Swamiji's voice came, 'Don't touch him! He is my child!', and the policeman disappeared.

Swamiji said the policeman was actually Yama, the god of Death.

'Now you don't worry. Go home.'

I woke up and it was early morning. 'What an amazing dream', I thought.

My mind was refreshed and peaceful. "

When Seenu awoke in the morning after his dream-vision,

the only words in his mind and on his lips were those of the mantra,

'Om Shivaya Shivabalayogendraya Parabrahmanaya'.

After having his morning bath he commenced his daily worship but found that only the words of this Guru Mantra came to him. Leaving home, he went to the house of the devotee who had offered to take him to the programme, partook of some food there and then along with his host-guide set off on foot towards the ashram where the programme was to be held. He felt uneasy and impatient as he was not sure that his guide was taking enough care to get to the programme on time and was concerned they might arrive too late. "As they walked on, Seenu's mind was enraptured" with the mantra which continually repeated itself in his head and he was really unaware of what the man was talking about, and even of his own replies.

When they finally reached the ashram where the programme was to be held, they found there were already thousands of people there with some devotees singing *bhajans* in a feverish pitch, while others danced around in an emotional state. His guide suggested they sit inside the hall but Seenu preferred, as was his usual habit, to sit quietly in a corner away from the noise and activity. Waiting, he tried to remain calm, but there was an inner urge which built up - an expectancy and also a certainty that He was the One he had been awaiting for so long. Something from within told him, "This is He who I have known since time immemorial."

" *Suddenly someone shouted, 'Swamiji is coming! Look at His car there!'*

With a boundless, peaceful joy I looked up. People were dancing feverishly and the bhajan *singing had reached its highest pitch - everyone there was excited.*

I prayed, 'I know You belong to all, but in the temple of my heart, deep in the consciousness, You belong to me and I belong to You, and You only.'

He came into my sight - my eyes met Him. That beautiful, lucky Chevrolet car pulled into the ashram compound. His blessed

Holy Mother was sitting with Him - a very humble and pious soul who simply served till the last breath of Her life.

Ah! That glow, aura of a dazzling light on His face. Anybody would simply fall in love and would be lost to the world. There was mad rush of devotees to see Him. They were crying, raising their folded hands in high, reverberating chants of

' Shivabalayogi Maharaj Ki Jai '

(Victory to Shivabalayogi Maharaj).

Slowly He alighted from the car. His beautiful jata *(matted hair) made one think that the great Lord Shiva Himself had descended on the Earth. Devotees were falling on the ground to touch His Feet. Due to His long* tapas, *His limbs were weak and so when He got down from the car He was supported by attendants who assisted Him in walking. Effortlessly, pushed forward by the crowd, before I could understand what was happening I found myself standing in front of Him. Gently I touched His Feet.*

I thought, 'These Feet of the Guru are going to be my lotus seat, the place where I have always lived.'

I looked up. He was watching. He smiled sweetly and gently - I was instantly drawn to Him, in fact I could feel that I was drawn back to Him. Then holding His hands to support Him, I walked along with Him. Nobody objected. All the time the mantra He had given me in the dream was in my consciousness.

Inside the hall He sat on a dais specially erected for Him. I sat in my place, at His Lotus Feet. I was simply watching Him. Then, this ' I ' disappeared and only He was there and everywhere. The mind was chanting ' Shivabala Shivabala Shivabala - Harabala Harabala Harabala'. After the Padapuja *(worshipping the Guru's feet) to Him, devotees sang* bhajans(devotional songs*) and then* arathi *(salute with light) was performed. Following this, devotees were allowed to come in a queue to touch His Feet. After they had touched His Feet, the attendants were sending the devotees out through another door, so that the rest in the queue could also then have their chance.*

I didn't want to go out; my eyes were fixed on Him; I didn't want to remove them. I don't know how long I stood like that. Suddenly I heard the devotee whom I had accompanied calling me to go in the queue and touch His Feet. I was at a distance and signalled ' No', but he misunderstood. He came closer and said , 'Don't be foolish - touch His Feet and receive His blessings.'

I said, 'I am at His Lotus Feet only and have already received His blessings.'

He looked at me, puzzled. After all the devotees went away, Swamiji glanced at me, then stood up and started walking to the car. I got up and holding His hands went along with Him up to the vehicle. Before He entered the car, I touched His Feet. He was watching. The car then drove Him away.

One could hear the reverberating chants of the devotees, 'Jai Shivabalayogi!' (Victory to Shivabalayogi). They were dancing. With folded hands they were touching their heads at all the places on the ground where He had placed His Lotus Feet.

He had gone and He was there too.
I was there and I had gone with Him too.

The mind was simply chanting the Divine Mantra He had given,

' Om Shivaya Shivabalayogendraya Parabrahmanaya '.

As he drove away, the ' I ' went with Him."

4

Sri Sri Sri Shivabalayogi Maharaj

God is never unjust to the creation. The Divine is the Ocean of Kindness. Whenever there is decline of *Dharma* (righteousness), the Divine comes to the rescue of the universe.

Whenever mankind is attracted too much to materialism it loses its mental and moral health, which results in increasing the miseries of mankind - tension prevails upon it, suffering spreads, both physically and mentally, and the people of the Earth suffer from dissatisfaction, depression, unhappiness. Doubts and fear, hatred and jealousy become the order of the day. The righteous always pray for peace and happiness, for love and universal brotherhood. Then the Divine Grace descends - and amazing, inexplicable wonders occur for the welfare of the universe. The righteous are protected by the Divine which appears on Its Own or chooses a worthy Child, a mighty Soul to carry out Its plan.

Such Great Ones, rising above all differences and weaknesses of mankind, use their powers and give their abilities and energies to aid humanity; by drinking bitterness They give Their love and tolerance. They take the sufferings of mankind and give Their Knowledge and Wisdom to enlighten the universe. Their approach is always Universal. They sacrifice Their lives for sake of the world. They become eternal, guiding and inspiring light to the universe.

So it was that the Divine came in the form of a young boy, born 'Sathyaraju' in the tiny hamlet of Adivarapupeta in south India on January 24th, 1935. Growing up Sathyaraju appeared a normal young boy in a family of weavers in a poor village; nothing appeared remarkably different about him as a child. He did however demonstrate a forthrightness and fearlessness in his dealings in the world and became the natural leader of his small group of companions.

Even as a small boy, he demonstrated courage and honesty and had enormous will power. He was always ready to face the moment instantly - ready to fight, whether it was poverty, blind faith, ignorance or injustice. When only eight years old, a Tantric[11] charlatan came to the village, trying to extort money from the poor villagers by threatening he would turn them into tigers and other animals by his magic powers. Where the other older boys and even village elders were scared of the Tantric, Sathyaraju felt it was just boasting and blind bullying from this fellow. Bravely he took the Tantric at his word, defying him to demonstrate these powers he claimed to have, by turning him into an animal if he was able - or be off! Sathyaraju told his elders, "Don't worry, even if I may have to die, people must know the truth about this boasting fellow" - such was his bravery and determination. Of course the 'magician' failed, and ran away.

Equally when he found the family trapped in the mire of poverty, made worse by the loss of his father when he was very young, he fought back. His insight showed him that he would need to use his mental skills as much as his physical abilities if he was to help the family out of their financial difficulties. Though working hard as a weaver even while yet a young boy, he thought that this by itself would not be enough to bring the family out of their poverty - others in the village also worked hard at their skilled work, but they still lived in tenuous circumstances. So he determined to start a small business even though he was the youngest of the family - only seven or eight years old - with an elder brother and two elder

---

[11] *Tantric* - A branch of the Hindu scriptures dealing with freeing one's mind in stages from the influence of the world, but sometimes wrongly applied to give 'magic' powers to the student.

sisters. His decision was instant and final, and he set about creating a business over the next few years.

His mother protested that he should not sacrifice his education, perhaps thinking that education might help him to escape poverty. But once decided, nobody - no power - could move Sathyaraju or shake his determination. So he started the business, and even though young, over time through his hard work and astute planning, he built up a useful income so that by the time he was in his early teen years he was the main breadwinner for the family.

Always very outspoken, commanding and outgoing by nature, he experienced an odd change coming over him when he reached the age of fourteen, preferring to quietly withdraw into a corner, and even losing his normally very healthy appetite, having little interest in the things around him. This uncharacteristic change in his demeanour persisted for several days and had began to trouble his mother, but she had other pressing concerns at the time, having to take her own father for eye surgery in the nearby town of Kakinada.

One afternoon Sathyaraju set off with his friends to play in the nearby Godavari River as he had done so many times in the past, but this day a special chapter in the Divine Play was about to unfold. On the way to the river, just as the boys were passing a grove of palmyra trees, three of the palmyra fruits fell down from the trees of their own accord. As a palmyra fruit can be broken into four equal pieces, and there were twelve boys in the group, Sathyaraju broke up the fruits and distributed the pieces to all those present.

He was about to start eating his share, when all of a sudden his body began to tremble and as he watched the palmyra fruit in his hand he beheld a light emerging from it and he heard the Omakara[12] emanating from inside it. As he continued to stare at the fruit, the Divine Light and Sound engulfed him in blissful waves

---

[12] *Omkara* - "Om" - the first sound from which all creation emerges.

so that his body ceased its trembling and his mind became calm and peaceful and he found further that as he watched, the fruit in his hand was replaced by a black Shivalingam[13]. Still drawn to watching the miraculous divine object in his hand, as he watched in awe the Lingam broke in half and from the midst of the Shivalingam a tall, handsome man in the attire of a Jangama Rishi[14] emerged and commanded him to sit into the lotus posture[15] and close his eyes. He then touched Sathyaraju in between the eyebrows and patted him on the head.

The boy lost all outer consciousness, absorbed in an enchanting vision of the same black Shivalingam which had manifested earlier in his hand.

His companions had not seen all this, being variously busy eating their spoils or playing amongst themselves. When they eventually turned to see their friend, they found him thus seated in his yogic posture, unresponsive to their calls. They tried various methods to 'awaken' him, even dropping him into the nearby river canal (the sacred river Godavari flowed by the hamlet), but when these all proved unsuccessful in bringing Sathyaraju back to worldly awareness, they fled back to the village to seek help from older sources. As his mother and grandfather were away in Kakinada, his uncle and a few others came to see what had happened and what could be done, but they themselves could also not awaken him, and even when one suggested beating the boy with a stick, it proved unhelpful in stirring a worldly awareness. Others eventually also came, hearing of the sudden and unusual change in the young boy's demeanour. These villagers were also unsure of what to do, some suggesting he was play-acting, some feeling he was possessed by a ghost, while others felt he was possessed by the local deity.

---

[13] *Shivalingam* - A symbolic representation of Lord Shiva, portrayed as an elliptical stone icon and used for ceremonial worship.

[14] *Jangama Rishi* - *Jangama* - A sect of wandering renunciates devoted to the worship of Lord Shiva. *Rishi* - Sage

[15] *Lotus Posture* - "Padmasana" - a cross-legged yogic posture commonly used for a stable bodily position during meditation.

One of the villagers however, astutely suggested he may have been transformed by a divine influence.

They carried him back to the village but when he did eventually return to a worldly awareness for a brief period, he walked back to the riverbank to the area where the transformation had occurred. Here he continued in unbroken meditation for the whole night and the next day. After a short break in which he took a light meal and had a short sleep, he then returned to his meditation and continued on day after day in this way for periods of about 23 hours a day with only a brief daily break for light bodily sustenance and to bathe.

Some in the village thought this was all a pretence and sham, and some even took the opportunity to cause mischief, some beating his body when he was in meditation, while one person even draped a burning kerosene-soaked cloth over his leg. Sathyaraju was so absorbed in meditation that he was unaware of these things except when he emerged from his meditative state, but eventually after some months, he decided to move to the village burial ground to avoid any of this unnecessary harassment, feeling that his tormentors might be reluctant to approach him so readily in such a place. While his troubles caused by the villagers was eliminated by this strategy, unfortunately here his body was attacked by insects and rodents, and even eventually bitten by a cobra, though divine intervention protected him from the serpent's venom. The Jangama sage came to him in visitations periodically to protect, guide, encourage and inspire him in his endeavours. After a year, a *dhyana mandir* (meditation room) was constructed for him and he continued his *tapas*, but he found he had lost the function in his limbs. He continued on thus for three more years, until the Jangama sage on one of his visits miraculously restored the use of his limbs, though the fingers of his hands remained bent and immobile for the rest of the body's life.

---

[16] *Samadhi* - Standstillness of the mind. A state in which the mind experiences no thoughts, but simply Awareness, being withdrawn into the Self.

After four years of intense *tapas* spent in *samadhi*[16] for about 23 hours a day, Sathyaraju, now referred to as a *Balayogi* (boy *Yogi*), experienced a vision of Lord Shiva as Shankara Bhagwan[17] and was subsequently initiated into *tapas* facing each of the four cardinal directions. He had already during these initial four years been facing East, so His Guru then directed Him in 1953 to turn towards the North and He continued this for about 21months. He then completed a very difficult period facing towards the West, during which time his body was afflicted with various severe maladies and He was again bitten by a cobra. He also experienced tempting visions during this phase of his *tapas* though they did not disturb His peace of mind. After a period of about 10 months facing the West, He undertook *tapas* facing the South for another 10 months thus completing the cycle of *tapas* facing all four directions over the eight year period. He then was directed to face towards the East again and continued that for a further 4 year period, during which time He was also instructed by His Guru to reduce His meditation period down to 12 hours a day, and to give *darshan* to those who came, and also to offer initiation into the meditation He Himself had practiced during his *tapas*.

In early June 1961, the *Balayogi* passed into *Nirvikalpa Samadhi*[18] in which state He stayed in unbroken continuity for about two months. Finally in early August He was aroused from this *samadhi* by His Divine Guru, the Jangama sage.

Smiling, the sage spoke, "You had a doubt about my true identity didn't you? Now watch me closely."

As He heard these words, the *Balayogi* witnessed a dazzling light, like lightning, flash forth from His Guru's body, and there standing in the same place he beheld the enchanting form of Shankara Bhagwan. This revealed to Him that His Guru had always been Lord Shiva, coming in the form of the Jangama Rishi to guide

---

[17] *Shankara Bhagwan* - A form of Lord Shiva as the Protector.

[18] *Nirvikalpa Samadhi* - *Samadhi* beyond time. Nirvikalpa samadhi occurs when the mind recedes totally (called '*manolaya*' in spiritual language) and thus merges with the infinite and eternal Self.

Him through his *tapas*. Shiva, and Parvati his consort who accompanied Him, then told the *Balayogi* that His *tapas* was now complete and that He was now free to roam about at will.

"You may now go wherever You like and do whatever You wish," They said.

Spontaneously He replied, "I had no desire of my own to do this *tapas*; it was under Your direction that I performed this. Now I have also no desire for anything and will do whatever You direct me to do."

Pleased with the answer, Lord Shiva then instructed Him to travel about as His Mission and through His *darshan* arouse the dormant spirituality of the people of the world, to help *sadhaks* (spiritual aspirants) in their struggles on the spiritual path through guidance and by initiation into *dhyana*[19], and give blessed *vibhuti* (sacred ash) to alleviate the sufferings of body and mind that trouble those of this world. Shankara Bhagawan then told Him that henceforth He should use the name "Shiva Bala Yogeshwara[20]". Later the *Balayogi* adapted this title to "Sri Sri Shiva Bala Yogi Maharaj[21]" as he felt the title "Yogeshwara" might be misconstrued by people to imply that He was equated with "Ishwara"(Supreme Lord).

Finally on 7th August 1961 after twelve years of austere *tapas,* Sri Shivabalayogi Maharaj melodiously chanted the holy "Om" and emerged from the *dhyana mandir* to bless with His *darshan*, the crowd of more than three hundred thousand who had gathered for this miraculous event.

He initially stayed in Adivarapupeta and an ashram, called Adi Ashram, was established there; but as His name spread, He

---

[19] *Dhyana* - "One's attention to" - The technique of meditation into which Shivabalayogi was initiated and into which He subsequently initiated others.

[20] *Shiva Bala Yogeshwara* - "Shiva" is the supreme Lord ; "Bala" is another name for Parvati, Lord Shiva's consort; "Yogeshwara" means 'Lord of Yogis'.

[21] *Shivabalayogi*- See Glossary

began touring first south India where an ashram which formed the administrative centre of His Mission was established in Bangalore, the capital city of Karnataka state and later another was established at nearby Ananthapur. He later travelled to the north of the sub-continent, establishing branch ashrams at Dehra Dun and Sambhar Lake.

Touring throughout India and also overseas He carried on the Mission assigned to Him, giving *darshan*, distributing *vibhuti* and giving *dhyana diksha* (initiation into *dhyana* meditation) to those who sort His spiritual guidance.

5

Three Long Years

When Seenu returned home after his mesmerizing first meeting with Sri Shivabalayogi, his mind was filled with thoughts only of Him; he was filled with Swamiji within. All he knew was that he wanted Swamiji. The mantra Seenu had been initiated into, 'Om Shivaya Shivabalayogendraya Parabrahmanaya', continued to entrance his mind.

He went immediately to his mother, still glowing within with the thoughts and memories of the vision of Swamiji's holy form and straight away began to pour out his heart to her.

" *I simply knew I had fallen in love with Shivabalayogi and other than that I couldn't explain or say anything. In my mind I kept repeating "Om Shivaya Shivabalayogendraya Parabrahmanaya". I returned home. I had forgotten about the crowds in the temple and the person who took me to meet Swamiji: only Swamiji was in my consciousness. I came home and declared to my mother that I had found my Guru and the time had come for me to leave home.*

She was stunned and remained silent for a while, then she said,

'I know this is playing on your mind, but what is your goal? What do you mean you have found your Guru? Why do you want to go to him? You could stay here and still do your sadhana *(spiritual practices). Why do you want to leave?'*

She was uncomfortable at the thought of me leaving. She

was naturally worried about my welfare - I was the youngest in the family and still a child of only 16 years, with no experience of the world. She asked if I knew Swamiji was genuine and if he had an ashram.

'You say, you have found Him, and that you want to go to Him. What do you mean by "I want Him" ? How do you know He is a genuine Yogi *? - He might not be so! He could be a fraud. Do you really know your target - what you are aiming for? How would you get on in an ashram? You have always been treated so well and gently here; you might find that it is too hard for you when you are away from us amongst the members of an ashram. Such a place could be very hard for you; can you face the challenges of life? You might find that you miss us and regret joining such a place. You can still stay at home and have Swamiji in your heart!'*

To all her questions, my newly-captivated mind could only answer,

'I simply want Swamiji. I don't know anything else.'

I felt totally and utterly drawn to Him, and I could see the faith - strong, quiet and complete - within me.

'I don't care if He's a chandahla (*charlatan*) *or a* Yogi. *I simply love Him and want to go to Him.'*

In this way the conversation went on for a couple of hours. I was trying to convince her that I wasn't a baby. I told her that for 16 years she had looked after me and now it was time I learnt to stand on my own two feet. Finally she said,

'I want you to wait for three years. If still after three years have passed your mind is unwavering in its determination to go to Swamiji, then I will send you with my blessings. Later, I don't want you to turn your back on your chosen path. You will go to his ashram only when I permit.'

On hearing this, out of respect for my mother's wishes, I agreed to wait the three years and also agreed not to run away during that time. "

Henceforth Seenu spent the whole day thinking of Swamiji

and reciting His mantra. At night he often dreamt of Sri Shivabalayogi. In one such dream, Seenu saw Swamiji emerge from inside a Shivalingam and then come and take His place on a dais. Seated there, He asked Seenu to sit beside Him and then turned to His mother who was seated beside Him, saying, "I have adopted him as my son", and she in turn expressed her delight. Swamiji then asked the boy to perform *abhishekam* (bathing the deity) to the Shivalingam, and pray to Lord Shiva that Shiva might fulfill his desire to be with Him. In the dream Swamiji would also repeatedly reassure Seenu that he would come soon, and would comfort him by saying,

"I have no objection to you coming to the ashram to be with me."

In another dream, Seenu found himself seated in a moving carriage, and on turning to the side, perceived Swamiji sitting beside him, steering the carriage.

Seenu asked, "When will You bless me to come to You?"

The Yogi smiled warmly and replied in a reassuring tone, "There is no need to worry. Just keep meditating and do *japam* (attentive repetition) of the mantra I gave to you. I don't have any objection to you coming to stay."

Pleadingly Seenu asked, "What is stopping You calling me now, if You have no objections?", to which his Guru replied tenderly, "You have forgotten your promise to your mother to wait for three years. After then, you will come to me."

In the same way in other similar dreams, Seenu would dream of Him sometimes sitting in a bus, while in another in a cave, and the conversations would always be similar - about coming to the ashram but needing to wait patiently at present. In one dream Seenu saw Swamiji sitting on a dais which was surrounded by four seats at an equal height off the ground. After Seenu prostrated to Him, Swamiji said, "These are to seat all four of you".

Seenu asked, "Who are the other three; where are they?", to which Swamiji replied,

"That is not to be revealed yet."

In another dream Seenu watched Swamiji performing *homam* in the four cardinal directions, and then He gave some *prasadam* (blessed food) to Seenu to eat. Often in the dreams Swamiji would be seen with His mother and Seenu speculated that may perhaps have been because he had seen Swamiji with His mother when he first saw Him in Mysore. All these dreams gave Seenu a great psychological thrust, strengthened his inspiration, gave him more confidence in achieving his goal, and fed his new-found love for his Guru.

As Swamiji was mainly staying in Bangalore while Seenu was living with his family in Mysore, it was not possible for the young aspirant to see Him all the time. But on important days such as Swamiji's birthday or His *tapas purti* (the anniversary of His *'tapas'*), with his mother's permission Seenu would travel to Bangalore by bus to attend the celebration functions at the Bangalore Ashram. The celebrations there would fill the whole day. From early morning until midday a *homam* would be conducted and Seenu would participate directly in that, or sit nearby and recite Swamiji's mantra mentally. Following the *homam*, a mass feeding would be held and this would involve the serving food to the thousands of people who gathered, including the poor and needy from nearby.

At about 2 pm Swamiji would commence giving *darshan* in the main hall, sitting quietly and peacefully on the dais. Just as when he had Swamiji's *darshan* for the first time in Mysore, the arrangement was for devotees to form a queue and thus enter the hall through one door, approach Swamiji sitting on the dais, take *namaskaram* (prostrate) and then exit through a second door. This enabled thousands of people to each have His precious *darshan* at such functions.

" *When one entered the room, the atmosphere generated by Swamiji's presence was electric; one felt as though they had entered Kailas - Lord Shiva's abode. At such sessions I would take my place quietly in the queue and on entering the hall I would find my attention magnetically drawn to Him. I was unable to see anything or anyone other than Swamiji; my eyes simply could not move away from the entrancing sight. Thus continuously watching Him as my place in the queue drew me closer to Him, held by the glorious sight and electric atmosphere, I would finally find myself standing in front of Him and would touch His feet with my forehead as* namaskaram. *Rising again from bowing at His Golden Feet, I would continue to watch Him sitting peacefully and majestically on the dais as I exited the room slowly. Then I would take a place in the queue again so that I could go back into the hall for His* darshan. *Like a mad person I would continue to return again and again for His* darshan *as long as the* darshan *session would continue - usually until about 11.30 or midnight.*

I recall at one darshan *session where Swamiji must have been aware of me coming in the line of devotees for His* darshan *again and again like a deranged person, He turned to one of His assistants and asked tenderly,*

'Does that boy have anything to ask?'

From my heart I instantly replied, 'I simply want to keep watching You.' "

When going about his daily tasks, throughout the day, he constantly repeated the mantra he had been given - "Om Shivaya Shivabalayogendraya Parabrahmanaya".

"*Whatever I did, this mantra became my best companion.*"

So in this way his beloved Guru Shivabalayogi came to sit as the absolute centre of his consciousness. Though shy to speak directly to the great *Yogi*, still Seenu wrote letters to Him from Mysore. He used to write down his feelings, his dreams and spiritual experiences in letters which he posted to Swamiji's ashram.

" *Occasionally I mentioned my name and address and*

received a reply written on Swamiji's behalf sending His blessings and encouraging me to do meditation, but usually I didn't mention my name or address. Whenever I wrote that I would like to come and stay at the ashram and included my name and address, I never received a direct reply. Swamiji would reply only through an assistant that I had to continue my sadhana *(spiritual efforts) and that my wishes would be fulfilled in due course."*

Although Seenu continued to see Sri Shivabalayogi at the ashram functions as much as was possible he had not been initiated into *dhyana* in these early encounters, so as his *sadhana* he would perform the recitation of Swamiji's mantra or simply would be lost in thoughts of Him. In December 1971 during the Indo-Pakistan War, Swamiji sat for *tapas* again for a period of 40 days, emerging on 24th January 1972. A function was held to celebrate His emergence from this *tapas* and taking the opportunity that presented itself at this auspicious time, it was on the following day, 25th January 1972, that Seenu was initiated by Swamiji into the sacred practice of *dhyana*.

This gave him the magical key, the philosopher's stone he had been searching for - the technique and technology whereby he could 'switch off the universe'. The earnest practice of *dhyana* now became the focus of his *sadhana* and thereafter Seenu would continue as before to go regularly in secret to the secluded Naagara Teertha cave in the Chamundi Hills outside Mysore which he had previously frequented, and here would now be absorbed in *dhyana* the whole day in this place of solitude. In the evenings he used to often go to the Ramakrishna Mission ashram which was near to his home and sit for meditation and sing *bhajans* with the ashram inmates. In this way he got a chance to be in the company of monks and so his *sadhana* continued while he patiently waited for the promised three years to come to an end.

During the earlier incident with him attempting to end his young life, when he was on the verge of death, Seenu's aunt had taken a vow to Lord Venkateshwara that she would perform his *poonal* (sacred thread) ceremony in the sacred Tirupati temple if he survived. The *poonal* is a symbol worn for centuries by the Brahmin community in India to show that they were qualified to undertake the study of the Vedic scriptures. Now that he had met his Guru and was sure he wanted to join Swamiji's ashram, he was concerned that if this 'unfinished business' was not addressed, the family might use the need to fulfill this vow as an excuse to call him back from the ashram once he had joined. So he determined to urgently fulfill this vow so that no excuse, no 'loose end', would remain by which he could be called back from his Guru's service once it had commenced. In order that the subject be brought up he hatched a clever plan. He started to grow a beard and felt that when it was noticed then someone in the family would ask him why he was growing it. This would give him the opportunity to say that as part of his endeavour to fulfill the vow which his aunt "had taken to Lord Venkateshwara, he would grow" the beard until he was installed with the *poonal* at Tirupati.

In May 1973 when his elder brother came on holiday from his work in Assam and saw the young Seenu sporting the beard, he naturally asked why he was growing the beard unnecessarily. Of course Seenu replied according to his plan that he had taken a vow that he would not shave until he went to Tirupati, performed the ritual shaving of his head (which is a common vow people often take when going to Tirupati), and was initiated into wearing the *poonal*. Hearing this, and being aware of his aunt's vow, the brother then organized the trip to Lord Venkateshwara's temple and the performance of the necessary rituals to have him installed with the *poonal*.

During these three years Seenu had been also studying botany at Mysore College. Now as the three year waiting period came towards it's conclusion (of which, of course, he was acutely aware), he thought that if he successfully completed the course then it might lead his family to start attempting to secure a job for him and so his dream of entering the ashram might vanish. The

Srinivasa in 1973 just before, and just after, visiting Tirupati for installation with *Poonal*

examination period was approaching and so to further ensure his future of entering the ashram, he resolved to make sure he did not pass the exam. "When the examination time came he entered the hall", wrote the sacred " OM " on the question paper but no answers to any of the questions - a sure plan for success at failure!

In May 1974, his brother wrote to the family in Mysore that he would be visiting from Assam in August, and that when he returned he planned to take Seenu and his mother back with him to Assam for a holiday. Though it wasn't directly mentioned, Seenu thought that the family might try to get him to take up a job there or some other activity such as further study. By now the promised three year period was coming to an end, so he thought that with this up-coming journey approaching, things might inadvertently progress such that he would still become entangled in a worldly life, with a job and even family responsibilities. Feeling that the situation was now urgent he thought to himself,

" *This could be my last chance to join the ashram. I must go to Swamij, and without any shyness, must ask Him if He will take me into the ashram.*"

So thinking, he wrote to the Bangalore ashram but received a reply that Swamiji was away at His ashram in Dehra Dun in northern India and was not expected back until September. This reply caused him great disappointment and despair, and he began to doubt that his wish would be fulfilled, thinking that events might conspire to take him away without meeting Swamiji. Distressed and anxious about his future life, and yet resolute in his determination, he felt he would take one last chance and try writing to Swamiji directly at the ashram in Dehra Dun. He resolved to accept that if he was truly destined to be with Swamiji then He would call him on reading the letter; but that if this letter did not yield a reply in his favour, then he would accept that he was destined to go away somewhere else (though he had no plans nor thoughts of what that would be). With firm intent and resolve he carefully framed the words of his letter, explaining that he had no interest in a worldly life, in studies or a career, and that he wished to come to Swamiji's Lotus Feet and stay in Swamiji's Bangalore or Adivarapupeta ashram. With prayers to Swamiji for His blessing he mailed the letter to the Dehra Dun ashram - and waited expectantly.

After 10 days, a letter of reply came to him from Dehra Dun. With hands trembling with a mixture of expectation and apprehension he opened the reply, to find that Swamiji's devotee Rumala Chennabasvaiah had written on His behalf, agreeing to take Seenu into the ashram,

"If you are interested you can come and live in Dehra Dun ashram. This is very ideal for your stay and *sadhana*. It is situated in the foothills of the Himalayas."

His dreams had been answered! How thrilled, relieved and excited he was!

Just as when he had his first meeting with Swamiji, Seenu again went to his mother, this time to tell her about the letter's contents. Boldly he announced to his mother, "I will go to the ashram. Swamiji has permitted me to go!"

This time his mother did not express shock. No doubt she was as conscious of the three year period as her son and must have been very aware of the passing of that time. She smiled at the news and seemed to accept it immediately.

"I knew one day you would definitely do this - but you were very naughty not to have told me when you wrote to Swamiji."

Vijay's young wife was staying in the house at that time as she had just recently delivered a child. While Seenu's mother's reaction had been so calm and measured, his sister-in-law's reaction was quite the opposite! On hearing the news, she started weeping and became distraught. After making efforts to calm her down, and considering the reaction the news created in the young lady, Seenu and his mother decided that it would be best not to tell the other members of the family at present, and that they would wait until the details were more finalized.

Now in the letter from the Dehra Dun ashram, Mr Rumala Chennabasvaiah had instructed Seenu that he should meet him in Bangalore and therefore the young aspirant excitedly left to contact Mr Chennabasvaiah there. On meeting him, Mr Chennabasvaiah told Seenu that Swamiji was happy to help him further his studies if he would like to follow that course; but Seenu politely declined, saying he really only wanted a monastic life. Hearing this, Mr Chennabasvaiah went on to tell him about the ashram in Dehra Dun, describing how it was a big, beautiful ashram in a quite, out-of-the-way area. He further told Seenu that Swamiji was due to come to Bangalore in September and that after that time he would be sent to the ashram in Dehra Dun.

So when Vijay finally arrived from Assam in August, some surprising news was awaiting him. But on hearing of his young brother's plans he did not oppose the idea, probably as he had been aware for some time of his brother's aspirations, and further because of the respect the children all had for their mother and that his mother was supportive of the idea. Seenu's mother was composed and at peace when speaking of the plan, saying, "If we force him to stay in the world, he will be confused."

So it was finally that at this stage, Seenu's life took its destined course.

With the family finally all having agreed to Seenu's decision to join the ashram and follow a monastic life, and having seen the family off on their trip to Assam, Seenu returned to the Bangalore home of Mr Chennabasvaiah in order to organize his joining the ashram. The following Sunday Mr Chennabasvaiah announced, "Swamiji has come back. Go and meet Him." So with excitement and anticipation Seenu went to the ashram for Swamiji's *darshan*, intending to identify himself and initiate the joining of Swamiji's service. But he found that again when he came into the *Yogi's* presence he was completely dumbfound - unable to speak directly to Him, so overwhelmed was he by the great *Yogi's* aura. He simply came away after having Swamiji's precious *darshan* but without having introduced himself as the one who had offered himself for Swamiji's mission.

" *When I returned, Mr Chennabasvaiah asked if I had spoken to Swamiji and organized any details of my joining Swamiji's service. When I told him that I had been unable to speak, struck dumb in His presence, he could only say in exasperation, 'What type of boy is this? How will they know who you are unless you tell them ?'*

In explanation I offered the comment, 'I was very shy', which Mr Chennabasvaiah seemed to accept.

'O.K., I will take you tomorrow' "

Unfortunately the meeting next day was not to be, as a phone call came from Swamiji before that visit could occur. Mr Chennabasvaiah was requested to accompany Swamiji immediately to Adivarapupeta on some urgent business, and so Seenu found that he would have to wait another 10 days before Swamiji was expected to return. Now a friend of Mr Chennabasvaiah's was also staying in the house at that time and he suggested to Seenu that he simply go out around the town during the day, have his food there, and return each evening to the house to sleep. The friend didn't realize, nor did Seenu inform him, that he had no money with him. Though Seenu's brother had given him 20 Rupees to see him to Bangalore and joining the ashram, that money had unfortunately been lost.

Having eaten no breakfast, and too shy to tell the man that he had no funds, Seenu left the house in the morning and ventured out onto the streets of Bangalore. Perplexed by his situation, aware he had to somehow exist for the next 10 days without any money, he wandered the streets quietly reciting Swamiji's mantra, wondering what he would do and who he might ask for help. By fortunate chance he was spotted by his maternal uncle who lived in Bangalore and who then naturally enquired what he was doing there. Still shy to tell his difficult situation Seenu casually replied that he was simply out for a walk. His uncle astutely thought there might be more to the story and so would brook no refusal in inviting Seenu back to his home for a meal. Through patient and persistent questioning he finally came to a fuller knowledge of Seenu's situation and offered the solution to his difficulties - that Seenu should come to his house daily for his meals, but return to Mr Chennabasvaiah's house each evening to sleep. Such a miraculous solution to his difficulties seemed to Seenu to be only possible as a manifestation of Swamiji's blessings.

After the 10 days were up and Swamiji returned, Seenu had expected to proceed with his arrangements further but he was again prevented from going to the *Yogi*. This time it was a serious viral fever which struck him abruptly and made it impossible for him to go to his Guru. Finding him so sick, his uncle took him back to his own home where he and his wife nursed the young boy constantly throughout the sickness, which lasted nearly three weeks. Finally Seenu came through this long ordeal only to find that October was almost over. Thus when fully recovered, Seenu approached Mr Chennabasvaiah again to arrange the introduction at the ashram and he told Seenu that he should go to the ashram to meet Mr Aradhya there, who would look after his needs. So it was finally on 1st November that Seenu again went to the ashram and met Mr Aradhya, who took him to Swamiji.

" When I was brought into His presence, Swamiji gently asked me, 'When do you want to go?' Having no personal preference or plans, but feeling I should give an answer, I simply replied, 'I can go in one or two days, or any time.' I was still shy to say that I had no money for the journey.

Swamiji continued, 'Come tomorrow. I'll give you a letter, and taking that letter you can go there.'

Taking His leave, I returned to Mr Chennabasvaiah's home, still with the issue of money unresolved. I was sitting quietly in the room for the rest of the day, praying constantly to Swamiji that He will understand that I have no money."

The following day he returned to the ashram to see Mr Adinarayanan in the office, who had organized the letter of introduction. Fortunately the gentleman also asked, "Have you made reservations to go?" which gave Seenu the opportunity to tell him that he had not purchased a ticket yet. Instructing him to wait Mr Adinarayanan went to consult with Swamiji and then returned ten minutes later.

"You should have told me if you're unable to purchase the ticket or don't have the means. If you come back tomorrow evening I'll have arranged it so you can go."

Returning as directed the next evening Seenu found Mr Adinarayanan had arranged a train ticket for 13th November to take him to Delhi and thence to Dehra Dun.

"If you come again on the evening of the 12th, we'll give you the ticket and letter then."

So about a week later, on 12th November, Seenu returned to the ashram and had Swamiji's *darshan* again. The *Yogi* instructed him,

"You have to look after the Dehra Dun ashram carefully. The people in the office will give you the ticket and also some money for any other expenses."

Hearing this, Seenu was greatly relieved that his monetary concerns had been dealt with - he had even been considering that with no money he might be compelled to walk the distance from Delhi to Dehra Dun! Then coming out to the office, while waiting for the office personnel to arrive, suddenly Swamiji's mother entered and seeing Seenu there, asked affectionately,

"Are you the one who is going to the Dehra Dun ashram?"

She appeared as excited as though she was talking about good fortune striking a son of her own. When Seenu replied affirmatively, she enthusiastically took him by the hand and led him out to the verandah, declaring,

"I must tell everyone that you are going to Dehra Dun."

Once outside, displaying him to those who were gathered there, she eagerly announced,

"Look! Swamiji is sending him to stay in Dehra Dun ashram. A *bhagyavan* (very fortunate) boy indeed!"

Having presented Seenu to the company assembled there she then drew him back to the office, enquiring where Seenu was staying at present. Knowing the place as a fair distance from the ashram and being aware that it was raining at the time, she felt that it would be best to provide money for him to travel back by proper transport. She called out loudly for Mr Adinarayanan, "Where has this man gone? It's late night - they should give some money for him to go."

Finding no success in locating help there, Swamiji's mother then went into Swamiji's rooms and then returned with His nephew, asking him to locate the ticket and give a further Rs100 to assist with his travels expenses to Dehra Dun. Having everything he needed for the journey Seenu was about to take leave of thc ashram when Swamiji's mother called back to him,

"Take Swamiji's blessings before you go. Tell Swamiji you have the ticket."

Entering His room, Seenu took *namaskaram* (prostration) to Swamiji. The great *Yogi* asked warmly, "Have you got your ticket and Rs100? O.K., now you can reach Dehra Dun peacefully. Practice *dhyan*, and look after the ashram carefully."

Empowered with this blessing, Seenu took leave of his Guru.

Thus on 13th November 1974 (which was *Deepavali* - a great celebration day in India), Seenu entrained for Delhi, a journey of two days' duration, and thence on to Dehra Dun by shared taxi. On 15th he reached the town-centre of Dehra Dun and subsequently caught a bus to travel to the ashram which was located on the outskirts of the town, on the road to the village of Rajpur, finally reaching the area of the ashram at about 10.30 in the evening. Asking the driver to let him disembark near the ashram, and thus relying on the driver's accuracy, he eventually found himself standing alone in the dead of night at the spot where the bus driver had left him, suitcase in hand, but unable to find the ashram itself. Peering through the darkness, Seenu saw a light in a nearby house compound and could make out the shadowy figure of the watchman standing there. On approaching, the watchman informed him that the ashram was two or three buildings down the road but refused to leave his post or help by guiding him or lending him any light. This left Seenu to tramp slowly and carefully through the darkness until, making out the dim light in the portico of Swamiji's ashram, finally found he had reached his destination and future home.

6

New Ashram Life

To assist the new ashram inmate, Swamiji had asked a lady devotee from Bangalore, Tilakamma, to stay at the Dehra Dun ashram for some time to help and guide Seenu in the daily tasks until he became accustomed to the place and the routine. The *Yogi* may have thought that after all, he was only a 20 year old young man with no experience yet of the world, living for the first time away from his family, unable to speak Hindi (the mother tongue of the region) and needing to learn the day-to-day skills necessary to be able to look after the ashram. Seenu found the ashram spacious and palatial, and its surrounds beautiful, with a serene atmosphere, clear views of the Himalayan foothills and surrounded by trees, greenery and the local paddy fields. He set about learning how to prepare food (Seenu at first didn't even know how to make a cup of tea), how to clean and maintain the building, and the procedure for the ashram *puja* (daily worship). He enjoyed everything he did and performed all the tasks with relish, feeling totally immersed in supreme bliss. For him it seemed as if he had come to Lord Shiva's abode.

Tilakamma told Seenu she had received a letter from the Bangalore ashram before his arrival informing her that Srinivas Dikshit would be coming to manage the running of the ashram. On seeing the name 'Srinivas Dikshit' she had formed an image in her own mind of a middle-aged man and so had been surprised when a 20 year old boy arrived - she hadn't thought that such a young person would want to come and stay in an ashram and take on the management responsibilities. After some weeks of showing him how to manage the ashram duties, one day Tilakamma informed Seenu she would soon be returning to Bangalore - which came as a great surprise to him as he had not been aware she would only be there a short time. For some time he was taken aback, realizing he would then have to manage the whole ashram himself.

Tilakamma and Seenu spoke to each other in Tamil, but if he needed to communicate with anyone apart from her then it was necessary to use either English or Hindi. His previous use of English had been fluent, but having lived in south India he had never spoken Hindi much previously. As one can imagine, this led to the extensive use of pointing and sign language in order to try to communicate with the local people.

In addition to these language difficulties, in the south of India it is usually warm, or hot, and arriving in November as he did, delivered him into his first experience of winter cold. He thus had no clothes suitable for this climate - on arriving at the ashram he had changed out of his pants and shorts (which he gave to the gardener) and had taken up the wearing of a *dhoti* (cloth wound around lower body) and light shirt (he had only two of each). Swamiji had written to the secretary of the ashram, asking him to purchase a sweater for Seenu to protect him from the cold and so with this he had to make do as best he could through the bitter winter of this region at the foothills of the Himalayan mountains. The sweater was the only clothing the ashram ever provided for him - after this he only ever relied on the occasional gift from well-wishing devotees.

Fifteen days after Seenu's arrival at Dehra Dun, a sudden phone call informed them that Swamiji would be paying a surprise visit the next morning! Initially His tour plan had been to visit Patna, but He had altered the plans to come unexpectedly to the Dehra Dun ashram. Of course Seenu was thrilled, even though the *Yogi* was only visiting for one day. On arriving and after settling in from His journey, Swamiji called Seenu to Him, enquiring affectionately,

"How do you like this place?"

The words leapt from Seenu's heart, "I think I am in Heaven."

Although Swamiji departed the following day, His visit had given the new ashramite great encouragement, inspiration and strength for his tasks ahead.

Seenu found that usually only the gardener had lived at the ashram until then, though devotees would come once a week for *bhajans*. The gardener, being the only person in permanent residence at the ashram until that time, had formed the opinion that he should be in sole charge of the ashram and so initially was not too happy when Seenu came to also stay there. He tried to unsettle the new ashram inmate by telling him 'cooked-up' stories such as, "This ashram is a very dangerous place - lots of wild animals roam around here. Don't ever step out, particularly during nighttime." But Seenu was not disturbed by these tales, and so the gardener went on to tell even wilder stories, such as how he had once been attacked and threatened at the ashram by armed gunmen. He would try to increase the story's drama by making his eyes wide in an over-acted way, declaring, "Oh they had big, big guns and they could shoot down people from miles away!" But Seenu simply smiled and ignored him.

The gardener felt his place at the ashram and his status and position were threatened by the new arrival and so, feeling insecure - as often happens in such situations - he imagined hidden political motives in the simplest actions of his imagined rival. When a few days later a new gas cylinder for cooking arrived to replace the empty one, seeing that Tilakamma was unable to fit it, Seenu came forward and simply connected it. Later when the gardener returned from his errands, he saw that the new cylinder had been connected by Seenu and became very unhappy, murmuring to Tilakamma, "Will this boy Seenu be staying here permanently?" It took a couple of days for his swollen, upset face to return to normal. Thus came Seenu's first encounter with the narrow-minded politics of the world.

In his new position of managing the ashram, Seenu started a program of daily *puja* and *arathi* (ceremony and worship), and also commenced daily *bhajan* sessions. Although he had been gifted with a beautiful singing voice, Seenu had not learnt how to play any musical instruments when young and so now set about trying to learn to play the harmonium and *dholak* (drum) so that he could accompany the *bhajan* singing.

" *Seated with a picture of Swamiji in front of me, like Ekalavya*[22] *I practiced each day.*"

Spending about an hour a day practicing, his innate musical skills flourished and his proficiency in playing the harmonium and *dholak* grew apace.

Among the devotees who came to the ashram, of particular note was the former Maharani Revati Devi of Patiala. The Maharani was a staunch devotee of Swamiji who had retired to Dehra Dun when her role as Maharani of Patiala had been completed. In her retired station, taking up spiritual practices under Swamiji's guidance she became known as Nagendra Swami and practiced *dhyana* for several hours daily. She would come to the ashram every day for a meditation session, staying for three or four hours, and leaving only after the evening *bhajans* were finished. Dressed in a white sari and with no footwear she presented the appearance of an ancient sage. She was in *mownam* (a vow of silence) and if she needed to communicate, would write in Hindi, so communication between she and Seenu thus presented some difficulties. However she was very affectionate to him, often stroking his forehead and smiling, and through Tilakamma serving as an interpreter he came to know that she felt he looked like her dear nephew. He heard from Tilakamma that she had offered to donate her bungalow to Swamiji but that Swamiji had told her

---

[22] *Ekalavya* - A character in the epic Mahabharata who wished to learn archery but could not be with his Guru, and so made a statue of him and learnt through his faith in the Guru.

that as He already had a large ashram in Dehra Dun, without manpower it would be difficult to look after other buildings as well. He had suggested that she could sell her bungalow, settle in the current ashram and use the money from the sale to further develop the present ashram. Seenu understood from Tilakamma that negotiations were underway to find proper buyers. Nagendra Swami invited Seenu and Tilakamma more than once to her home where she affectionately fed Seenu from her hand as one would a favoured child.

Each day when she came to the ashram for meditation Nagendra Swami would write short notes in Hindi to Tilakamma and one day Tilakamma told Seenu that Nagendra Swami had informed her that she had been threatened by some people, telling her that she shouldn't give the bungalow to Swamiji and should cease her *mownam* (silence) and start talking again. One day in January 1975, she left the ashram as usual after the evening *arathi* but forgot to take *prasad* (blessed food) with her. When Seenu pointed this out, Tilakamma casually answered that they could always give it to her the next day. But, unexpectedly, she did not come as usual that following day. Even though it was raining, Seenu was surprised she didn't come as it was always her habit to attend, no matter what the weather.

So it was a deep shock for Seenu and Tilakamma when they heard the dreadful news that Nagendra Swami had been killed during the night by some unknown assailants. For Seenu she had seemed a very noble lady who was totally devoted to Swamiji and deeply serious in her dedication to the practice of *dhyana.* Later, from listening to various comments from people, Seenu heard that her property was the reason for her being killed - to stop her donating it to Swamiji.

After this shocking incident, Tilakamma started saying that she was receiving frequent threatening phone calls demanding that they vacate the ashram and she naturally became quite distressed by this. Gradually this situation developed to the point where she would sometimes awaken screaming in the middle of the night saying that she had experienced a vision of Nagendra Swami and had seen her covered all over in blood. Distressed as she was, Tilakamma suggested that they should both leave the ashram for their own safety and further because if they were injured, or even killed, it would damage the reputation of the Mission. She also suggested that other devotees sleep in the ashram overnight to create greater safety. Because she was elderly Seenu did not argue or openly oppose her view, but felt that he should not leave like that, thinking,

"Why should I leave this ashram as long as Swamiji has permitted me to be here? Even if I am killed it would be like I was a soldier dying on the battlefield, doing my duty."

Though Tilakamma was obviously disturbed, Seenu himself felt no doubt or confusion about what he should do - he was firm in his plan to stay in the ashram. After a few more days Tilakamma began applying pressure to Seenu to leave for Bangalore so that he could inform Swamiji directly of the dire situation in Dehra Dun. She herself also planned to leave. As she was an elderly lady Seenu would usually have followed her instructions out of respect, so for a short time he felt confused as to whether he should follow her advice or not. His natural inclination however was to stay on at the ashram even if Tilakamma herself chose to leave. He also thought that if he did leave Swamiji might get annoyed at him for leaving without His permission. Therefore Seenu asked her to give him a few days during which time he would write to Swamiji to convey the circumstances at the ashram and request His guidance as to what he should do. He told Tilakamma,

"If Swamiji feels the same as you are feeling and asks me to leave, then obeying the Guru's order I can leave peacefully."

Apart from his obedience to Swamiji, Seenu had a further reason in not wishing to leave in that he had promised his mother that he would not go back on the path he had chosen. He also was actually unsure whether Tilakamma might not have even created a sort of phobia from her own panic and imagined the threatening phone calls.

A reply came immediately from Swamiji in a letter instructing Seenu that he should not leave under any circumstances and telling him that He would bless and look after him so that no one would touch even a single hair on his head. Now freed of any slight confusion, Seenu was fully confident in staying on at the ashram and would not contemplate leaving under any circumstance.

During those days, sometimes odd things would happen amongst the devotees in the name of *bhava*[23] (trance). At one *bhajan* session, one lady from a nearby village who had been in the habit of coming for *kirtan* (devotional singing) suddenly stood up, started pulling at her hair so that it was standing out on end, dancing in a ferocious manner and apparently claiming to be Nagendra Swami, shouting,

"These people who killed me will come here and kill you also! You must leave this place!"

Tilakamma was very distressed and disturbed at this but Seenu didn't take it seriously, thinking that it was just the lady's own imaginations playing out. Another lady who was a servant of one of the devotees also began to show this 'Nagendra Swami *bhava*'. She used to come and stay in the ashram and assist with the cooking, and Tilakamma encouraged her as she was quite helpful with the preparation of the food.

Now this lady had become a little attracted to the handsome new inmate of the ashram.

As an astute judge of people Seenu was concerned about her intentions and his disquiet was shown to be justified when after a few days, an odd episode occurred. At one meal the lady was forcefully insisting on Seenu eating more of the *chapatis* (flat bread) she had cooked but Seenu quietly but firmly declined, saying

---

[23] *Bhava* - '*Bhava*' refers to the mood or attitude of mind, the emotional feelings of the mind. The depth of the *Bhava* experienced by devotees varies with devotees' differing temperaments and spiritual maturity. The development of this strong emotional feeling in the mind will tend to focus the mind's attention, making it easier for a *sadhak* to then go into *dhyana*, which was the main focus of Swamiji's ministry.

simply that he was already full. The lady was very displeased at this rebuttal and the next morning suddenly adopted a strange countenance and manner, shaking her head in an odd way and speaking commandingly to Tilakamma,

"I am Nagendra Swami. I am very displeased as last night I came in this body and Seenu refused to accept *chapatis* from me."

While Seenu understood that the lady was only pretending, poor Tilakamma with her mind already in a disturbed and impressionable state, became distressed and started scolding Seenu and apologizing to 'Nagendra Swami',

"Please forgive him, Nagendra Swami. Now what do you want him to do?"

"I want you to punish this boy and get him to prepare a nice cup of milk and bring it to me."

Following these instructions Tilakamma insisted that Seenu prepare some milk and bring it for 'Nagendra Swami'. Seenu felt he needed to take some action to quieten this lady down, so going to the kitchen he heated the milk nicely but instead of adding the usual sugar he thought instead of adding salt to the drink. Returning to 'Nagendra Swami' and playing along with the pretence he offered the milk to her,

"Nagendra Swami please accept this milk."

Pleased with this the lady took the glass and drank the milk eagerly, but then suddenly struck by its saltiness, she was unable to swallow it and abruptly spat the milk back into the glass. She never troubled Seenu again and in fact left the ashram after a few days. Soon Tilakamma also left for Bangalore.

Hence the young Seenu found himself thousands of miles from his family, amongst people he didn't know, unable to speak the local language, unschooled in cooking skills and where a violent murder had been recently committed. Yet his immense faith in his Guru and the great strength of his character guided him through this period and he was calm and sure throughout; no doubt assailed him. He was simply content to be able to offer his services to

Swamiji in whatever way that circumstances might allow.

About one month after Tilakamma left, Swamiji sent a man from Karnataka to Dehra Dun to look after the cooking and generally help in the running of the ashram. Though at first he appeared to be a good person, it soon became evident that he suffered a short temper and seemed to easily misunderstand people and come into conflict with the devotees who attended the ashram *kirtans* and programs. Even at such a young age Seenu felt one working in the Mission should have a lot of patience in dealing with the public, as only then could one offer service to them as part of the Mission. Within the first month Seenu found this man also had a peculiar habit which at first he didn't understand. The man would talk about '*bhang*'[24], saying that it was useful in meditation and could help one to go deeper into the meditative experience. Seenu wondered if such a thing was really possible with a physical substance; if that were so, why would the sages do hard, vigorous sadhana to realize the Self when they could just use this *bhang*?

One day another man who attended the ashram as a devotee told the helper that he could bring some *bhang* if he would like and of course the new ashram worker was very keen. So the next day the men prepared *pakoras* (fried savouries) to which they added some *bhang* and then offered some to Seenu. Fortunately, seeing this, the gardener who was staying in the ashram called Seenu aside and warned him,

"If you eat the *pakoras* laced with *bhang* you will have a blissful experience and the sensation of flying in the air, but this is a highly intoxicating substance."

Now when gardener said "intoxicating substance", Seenu was shocked and alerted. His father had always been very adamant that such things were harmful to the health and had trained his children against the use of any intoxicants. He had instructed them that these things were harmful to the health of the body and also

---

[24] *Bhang* - A crude form of opium

suppressed the brainwaves and the nervous system's functioning; they might give a temporary pleasure for the mind but were very harmful to the brain's and nervous system's health and would make a person unable to even perform their normal daily duties.

Knowing this, Seenu declined the laced *pakoras*, "I'm sorry, I cannot have this."

Nonetheless the man and the devotee both ate a plateful of *pakoras* between them.

The devotee who supplied the *bhang* seemed unaffected and after some time left the ashram to return home (later Seenu came to know that he frequently used of all types of intoxicants and thus was less affected by them). But the ashram helper then sat for meditation about 3 o'clock in the afternoon. Generally one hour was the time most of the devotees would sit for *dhyana* but this man was still sitting after many hours had gone by, even when the arathi was performed at 7 o'clock in the evening and indeed was still sitting at 11p.m.. At this point Seenu became concerned. He had never seen someone in meditation for such a long period and was unsure what could have happened to the man - was he unconscious? Coming closer and examining him more closely, Seenu could see that his eyelids were moving violently and he was forcefully grinding his teeth.

Not knowing who else to call, and having found his guidance invaluable earlier in the day, he called the gardener to come and see what had happened to this man - was he in deep meditation or what had happened? Seeing the man still stilling there "meditating" after so many hours, the gardener gave a hearty laugh.

"Don't worry. Make some tea and bring it here and I'll show you what will happen now."

Seenu returned with a cup of tea, which he presented to the gardener. Turning to the man, the gardener commanded, "Lie down!"

To Seenu's surprise this man who had been in a meditation posture, unmoving for hours, simply lay down as if he was under a hypnotic spell.

Again the gardener spoke, "Hey brother, get up and have a cup of tea."

Seenu's fascination began to turn to amusement as the subject sat up and drank the proffered tea. The gardener again directed him, "Lie down and go to sleep", and of course his subject again obeyed! With the man now lying down and apparently sleeping, the gardener explained to the young novice,

"He must have had an overdose of *bhang*. Don't worry. He'll be OK when he wakes up in the morning - you go now and have your sleep."

The next day a little after midday the man finally got up, but his eyes were bright red and his movements unbalanced and sluggish. He asked for some buttermilk so Seenu brought some for him to drink, to help him revive.

This use of *bhang* was repeated on several occasions and Seenu became disturbed about such things occurring in the ashram. On Swamiji's next visit Seenu explained his concerns to his Guru and hearing of these goings-on the *Yogi* scolded the man and ridiculed him, saying that if he was going to live in the ashram he must stop this bad habit. Swamiji declared it a very wrong practice which would never help in true mediation and would instead induce more mental turmoil, greed and anger in the mind. Later on another occasion, when another devotee further asked Swamiji, "Don't the legends say that Lord Shiva uses *bhang?*", He became furious and ridiculed such beliefs. Then He jokingly derided the question, "If you are going to have *bhang* on the pretext that Lord Shiva does too, then Lord Shiva also drank *halahara*[25] poison - why don't you drink that also? These are very wrong stories, written by selfish people who have not experienced any spiritual truth or anything about God. Lord Shiva has nothing to do with these things. This is all just human weakness."

---

[25] *Halahara* poison - Refers to a legendary story in which Lord Shiva drank a poison which welled up from the stirring of the ocean, symbolising the destruction of the mind's acquired habits by the process of meditation.

Swamiji further advised Seenu to be careful and that these practices and their exponents should be vigilantly avoided. He told His disciple to be watchful as some sadhus also took this substance by smoking it through a fire. The device used for this made a resonant noise and mimicking the sound, Swamiji referred to it as the "gudi-gudi" habit.

"Be careful. If these people come here, simply send them away."

This advice reminded Seenu of something he had seen earlier in his life when he was living in Mysore. At that time he had gone with a friend to the Chamundeshwari Temple in the hills outside the town and one of the priests there, knowing of his interest in spiritual matters, advised him that in a cave in the hills a great realized soul stayed and offered, "I'll take you to him." So they set off together and when they reached the cave they found an anchorite there and Seenu saw him smoking something from a long pipe with the other end in a campfire. The priest explained to them,

"This *avadhuta* (naked ascetic) is totally God-intoxicated. Even when he walks on the roads he is totally unaware of the surroundings and is in his own world, absorbed in God."

Currently Seenu saw that the *avadhuta* stood up and started dancing in a very odd way as though he was heavily drunk, and then fell to the ground and started rolling about. Seenu was unimpressed with this and was not attracted to take him as a Guru. He had not seen descriptions of any such behaviour or experiences in the writings and teachings of Adi Shankaracharya, Ramakrishna Paramahamsa, or Ramana Maharshi and so did not feel they were valid spiritual expressions. It was only later in Dehra Dun, when he had his experiences with the ashram helper using *bhang* that he understood what the *avadhuta* of Chamundi was really doing. It made him feel very sad that people get so easily misguided by these sorts of things and lose track of the real *sadhana* and the true goal, and also that other gullible people of the world then easily get carried away and wrongly think of them as God-Realized *avadhutas*.

7

Life with Swamiji

The ashram was a huge building donated to Swamiji's trust by Maharani Kailash Kumari Devi of Patna, who Swamiji always called "*Ma*" (mother) and the ashram attendants referred to by the respectful term of "*Mataji*". She and all her family were always affectionate to Seenu and Mataji seemed happy that Seenu had come to the Dehra Dun ashram, aware of his sacrifice in leaving his home to serve Swamiji's Mission. Whenever she came to Dehra Dun she would always visit and enquire after his welfare. Swamiji's Dehra Dun ashram was only one of several held in His name and so He therefore travelled a lot from place to place, but usually came to the Dehra Dun ashram once each year. Seenu thus had many months of the year when Swamiji was not in residence in which the daily routine of the ashram was quite quiet and he established a daily routine of *sadhana* during these times.

In the early morning he would awaken and meditate for a couple of hours and then about 6.30, after a cup of tea, he would dust and clean the upstairs hall and rooms. Following the cleaning he would have a light breakfast, bathe and perform worship at Swamiji's shrine and then help cook lunch. The man from Karnataka who Swamiji had sent to help with the cooking and running of the ashram, stayed in the ashram for six or seven years before being sent on to Swamiji's Hyderabad ashram, and so while he was still there Seenu would help him in the morning with the cooking of lunch. After the lunch Seenu would read the Yoga Vasistha during the afternoon and then practice an hour of meditation, before the evening *puja* (worship) and about an hour of *bhajans*, during which some devotees would also come and participate. His evening meal he would cook for himself, as the man from Karnataka was often 'busy' in the evenings with the habit which was mentioned earlier, and then following this he would again meditate for another couple of hours before retiring to sleep.

Most years Swamiji would come to the Dehra Dun ashram during His north India tour after visiting His centres in Agra and Sambhar Lake, usually staying in Dehra Dun for about two or three months. During His stay, devotees would visit from both north and south India and the whole ashram would take on a festive atmosphere. Throughout these periods the pace of work for Seenu was constant and often frantic, but his great attachment and dedication to his Guru's service meant that he enjoyed every part of his work and service to Swamiji. Although when the ashram was quiet (when Swamiji was not in residence) he had a room downstairs which he used as his bedroom, when Swamiji was present, with so many devotees coming to stay, Seenu vacated that room for the use of others and simply slept in the upstairs hall behind Swamiji's room on the concrete floor.

The daily pattern during these months would usually be that Swamiji would awaken him at 3.30 by poking him with the stick He carried on His walks, "Come Seenu, time for a walk." After a quick bath he would prepare the morning milk for Swamiji and also some tea for any devotees who might also accompany Swamiji on His early morning walk. It was not every time that others would accompany Swamiji and so often Seenu had the opportunity to walk with Him alone. The practice was to walk out through the fruit orchard at the rear of the ashram campus and then down the steep hill behind the ashram to the riverbed at the base of the slope.

As Swamiji's limbs had been so affected by His *tapas* occurring during His growing teenage years, He required support during this trek particularly when wending His way down the steep, winding path on the hillside. Seenu took great delight in providing that support, which meant he would have to walk in front of his Guru as they moved down the slippery path in order to brace their descent and Swamiji would usually seem to take special care to scold him during these hikes and make him nervous. That seemed to be Swamiji's way constantly if He was with Seenu while he was attending to any task - to be scolding him for what he had done, for what he had not done, for what he might do or might not do and Seenu found a nervousness develop in him sometimes due to these chidings. Of course the nervousness itself would sometimes cause him to then commit the very mistake he was trying to avoid, which would of course lead to further teasing or scolding from his Guru. Often during these walks Swamiji would also loudly announce the local gossip, particularly about the neighbours who were within earshot, and this caused further worry to His disciple. But all this meant that nothing was hidden between the two in their precious relationship and only further strengthened the great intimacy that was developing in their association.

With the group reaching the riverbed, all would sit there for some time - except Seenu who would have the task of again scaling the steep hillside to the ashram, where in the kitchen he would prepare tea for Swamiji and the devotees who had accompanied Him, which he would then pour into several thermos flanks. Ladened with these thermoses over his shoulders, a bucket of water in one hand and glasses for the tea in the other, he would set off down the hill a second time to deliver the refreshments. Throughout this procedure Seenu would be rushing to prepare everything as quickly as possible, aware that Swamiji may launch into one of His teasing scoldings, "Oh where is he; why's he taking so long? He must be feeding himself in the kitchen instead of making the tea!"

Returning from this morning walk Swamiji would sit under a tree in the orchard and send Seenu into the ashram to clean His bedroom and the hall. Seenu would then make the necessary preparations for Swamiji's oil massage so that when the *Yogi* returned to his room, some of His close devotees could perform a massage of His body. Following this Swamiji would insist that those devotees be fed and Seenu would assist in preparing the breakfast. Though the man from Karnataka was supposed to be the main cook, he was not happy in preparing food for devotees and would see it as his task to prepare food only for Swamiji Himself, so in turn Swamiji insisted that all the devotees in attendance should be fed in front of Him to ensure they were given proper food.

With the devotees thus fed, it was then time for Swamiji to bathe but because His hands were not flexible due to the years of *tapas*, it was necessary for others to help in that task. So Seenu and sometimes others would bathe Him before the *Yogi* finally sat for His breakfast meal. As he was attending to all the other devotees or to Swamiji Himself, Seenu would thus only eat breakfast after all the others were finished.

Following this, the rest of the morning was then mainly taken up by answering the mail which would arrive about 10 o'clock. It usually consisted of about 30 or 40 letters sent by people from all over India writing to ask Swamiji for His blessings or asking for guidance or assistance with various problems and troubles. Seenu's job was to read all these letters to Swamiji and usually He would ask those present that they send a reply, "Write My blessings to them, and assure them it will be alright." After all the mail had been read it was time for Swamiji's lunch which would finish about 4pm. The replies to the morning mail were written throughout the afternoon. Various devotees would undertake to write the replies, but where most only wrote a simple one or two lines offering Swamiji's blessings and reassurance, Seenu found he wished to write the replies assigned to him in more detail and with more affection, remembering the times when he himself had written to Swamiji after the first meeting. He would try to expand the reply to a longer missive, directing the recipients to have faith and devotion and remember Swamiji's name, and reassure them that Swamiji had conveyed His blessings.

With lunch finishing, Seenu would again bathe and then prepare the hall for the evening program at which devotees would come for initiation into *dhyana* (meditation). On such occasions Swamiji would initiate those who came by touching Seenu in between the eyebrows and then ask Seenu to instruct the devotees on the technique and in turn touch them between the eyebrows as initiation. The new initiates would then practice *dhyana* for about one hour together with others who had already received the initiation on previous occasions, before the program would continue on with the singing of *bhajans* for a couple of hours. With the *bhajans* finished, *arathi* (salute with light) was performed before *prasad* (blessed food) was distributed to all those present. After this, devotees were allowed to come and ask Swami any question they wished and as Swamiji spoke mainly in Telugu, Seenu would act as an interpreter between them and Swamiji would convey His blessings by giving *vibhuti* (sacred ash).

With the evening program completed Swamiji would withdraw to the balcony outside, typically with some close devotees, and Seenu would serve His dinner there. After some time the other devotees would progress downstairs to have their own dinner and retire to bed. Many a day this left Seenu alone with his Guru as Swamiji paced the balcony, and at this precious and glorious time with Him alone Seenu could ply the great *Yogi* with any queries he might have.

Swamiji always spoke of all religions as equally honourable, saying that it was only human selfishness and folly that made them appear different. He never wished to be referred to as a "religious teacher", saying instead that, "I am a *Yogi* - above all religions, not limited to any one place or one group, or any one type of creature. *Yogis* are for all humanity and even bless other creatures as well. Anyone, anywhere can receive Our blessings." He spoke of the Self and how important it was to know who You are and urged that this was possible through *dhyana*. He talked also of equality among human beings and never liked the artificial divisions which society creates - such as wealth, caste or creed. Having experienced discrimination based on such man-made criteria as a child, He always treated all alike. With his Guru conversing like this, often until midnight, Seenu would relish the opportunity to be in His blessed presence and at this time Swamiji would sometimes sing (which He did not do at the public programs) and his poignant rendition of *Lingashtakam* (song in praise of Lord Siva) would sweeten the ashram night air, frequently with Seenu accompanying Him on the harmonium. Seenu would always wait until Swamiji directed him to go to bed and so it was often midnight or 1, or even 2 o'clock before Seenu went to sleep in the hall with Swamiji returning at 3.30 to awaken him for the new day's cycle of work.

While this may sound very exciting and even romantic - and indeed it was - when the pattern was repeated day after day for weeks and months with only a few brief hours' sleep each day for the whole of Swamiji's stay, the pure physical demands on Seenu were extreme. Yet he was thrilled as always to be of service, relishing the rare opportunity he had been given in having a chance to serve Swamiji and the Mission, driven by his great faith in, and love for, his Guru. The physical drain was naturally accompanied by an emotional and mental strain as well. Such a situation would normally magnify the flaws in anyone's personality and that combined with Swamiji's peerless eye for finding faults in His disciple would normally create a perfect situation for showing one's character shortcomings. Yet Seenu's great strength and depth of character, innate wisdom and dedication to serving his Guru saw him easily through these demands.

The stern discipline and frequent criticism the Guru applied to His disciple was simply a measure of Seenu's openness to his Guru's direction and guidance. "You are perfect, but I shall make you more perfect", Swamiji was sometimes heard to say. From the first day he had seen Him, Seenu had felt deeply attracted and attached to Swamiji. When he entered Swamiji's service, this grew such that whether Swamiji was being sweet and affectionate or shouting and scolding, it made no difference to his disciple - Seenu always felt of Swamiji as his own. Swamiji would often scold him severely - sometimes even when there was no fault on his disciple's part - but still Seenu would simply accept whatever his Guru said or did; he never tried to explain or excuse anything he did.

" *Though He appeared tough on the outside, He was very affectionate from the inside. He loved me like a mother; always trying to teach the inner truth of spirituality and also trained me like a tough father to be perfect in everything. His main emphasis was on losing the ego. He used to test the ability of the mind by always trying to find some fault or other. Sometimes even if the fault was not real He would still mention it.*

While His methods may have appeared harsh to the outside observer, it was simply that He cared so much for me that He wanted to make me as refined as possible and so wished to remove any small blemish or weakness. Being straight-forward, blunt in His approach by nature and knowing I had authorized Him to remove my ego, He set about the task with great care and love, but without restraint. Many may have misunderstood His approach to me, which to an outside observer may have appeared harsh at times.

It is like when a sculptor is fashioning his creation, he approaches the coarse rock and vigorously hammers away with the mallet and chisel. To someone looking on who does not know the art of sculpting, it may appear a very harsh act of beating the stone violently; but finally when the beautiful carved figure emerges from the original rock, the great skill of the sculptor can finally be appreciated. "

Thus Seenu never felt anything was wrong in Swamiji admonishing him; in fact sometimes if the scolding was not occurring he would feel odd as though something was missing. In this way, an immensely valuable relationship was built up between Seenu and his Guru in a very committed way; over time it developed that no barrier existed between the Guru and the disciple, no facade of appearance. Seenu always felt very secure at His Lotus Feet so that even though Swamiji might be reprimanding him, Seenu felt very comfortable inside and took it as a great spiritual blessing.

Swamiji was very fond of feeding devotees and would insist on conducting *annadannum* (mass feedings) on occasions at which thousands would gather. He once explained, "Look if you eat at a restaurant then it is simply food. But when the food is offered to God it becomes *prasadam* (blessed food). During mass feedings if someone contributes even a little food to the occasion, that person's *bhava* (the emotional feelings of the mind) will be purified with the thought, 'May my little contribution be helpful in the feeding of the poor and needy,' and the volunteers who work in the preparation and serving of the food will do their work out of devotion to God and Guru, so they are also purified in their *bhava*. And all those who partake of the food shouldn't think of it as ordinary food but the *mahaprasadam* (great blessing) of the Guru's Grace."

Swamiji was equally fond of feeding those near Him.

" *When we sat with Him, He was constantly feeding us with some* prasad. *If I was sitting with Him, He would love to feed me carefully with any item that might be available. If He gave something I could not say 'No' and so as I sat He would often feed me continually.*

I used to think He liked to feed me, and He must have thought I liked to eat."

One incident regarding food was particularly well remembered.

In the evening after escorting Swamiji to the dais for *darshan*, Seenu would return to his Guru's room to fill up all the buckets and tubs with water (the supply was such that the water came for only a short period in the evening and so it had to be kept stored for later baths). Devotees would often bring sweets as an offering to Swamiji and during this evening period, when alone in the room, Seenu would sometimes take a snack of any sweets which might have been left in the room. Once a devotee had brought a box of coconut sweets and when Seenu would return to the room for the water routine, he would take the opportunity to eat one sweet from the box each day. After about ten days of doing this, Seenu suddenly realized there were now very few pieces left in the box and so thinking that Swamiji would notice if he took one when only so few were left, he decided it was best if on this day he wouldn't take any. After the *darshan* session was over Swamiji returned to His room, suddenly looked at the sweet box, and turning to another devotee announced,

"Hey, today he has not touched any of the sweets!" and gave a roaring laugh.

Looking at Seenu he asked, "Hey. Do you think I did not know you were taking a piece every day? When I went out to the hall I used to count the sweets, and when I came inside one piece every day used to be missing. But today when I counted nothing was missing." Seenu prepared himself for a scolding from his Guru, thinking, "Oh, this is it!", but the *Yogi* simply roared again with laughter.

Seenu would simply carry on his tasks – whether Swamiji was physically present at the ashram or not – engrossed in thinking of his Guru or reciting His name, lost in Swamiji's *bhava* (single-pointed focus of the mind on Swamiji). He would take great care in preparing items and equipment for use around the ashram, taking great pains to cover all likely events where possible. Each morning when Swamiji went out for His early morning walk at 3.30 He would need a torch to light the way and prior to one particular visit by his Guru, Seenu had readied it for Swamiji's use and had checked it frequently to make sure it was working properly; in addition he kept a second torch as a back-up in case the first one failed for some reason. One morning as Swamiji was about to go out for His walk, He was trying to switch on the torchlight but the light would not work, so Seenu took it and himself checked it thoroughly - flicking the switch from off to on repeatedly, turning it over to check it was screwed together properly, twisting it in various ways here and there until he found there was no way he could make it work. As he had only checked the torch recently and it had worked perfectly well at that time, he simply felt exasperated - until he remembered there was the second torch kept as a back-up for just such an occasion. So he assured Swamiji that he would run downstairs and fetch that light, feeling relieved that he had covered just this sort of event. Returning triumphantly with the second torch, he passed it to Swamiji, but as the *Yogi* held the torch to turn it on, it abruptly fell into pieces in His hands! Of course this gave Swamiji a chance to scold him, "You never keep anything ready. You always do such nonsense things! You'll make Me fall over in the dark and break My leg", and so on in this manner - unrelentingly as they set off on their walk, with Swamiji continuing the tirade and Seenu simply walking quietly beside Him with his head bowed. Having taken all human pains to prepare adequately, all Seenu could do was to surrender to the Divine.

When Seenu was working on a task, Swamiji would tease or scold him to make him feel nervous and then enjoy the fun – even if Seenu was already doing something, Swamiji would tell him that he should do it faster and so again he would become nervous. For His early morning walk Seenu would dress Him in socks and shoes, with a *dhoti*(waist cloth), belt and shirt, and Swamiji would often joke that whereas other people dressed up fashionably to go into town, He dressed up very fashionably to walk in the forest! A few times, in his haste and nervousness, Seenu mistakenly put the left shoe on the right foot, and vice versa. But the *Yogi* would simply go off for His walk unnoticing. Eventually after walking all the way down the hill, one of the devotees would notice the error, pointing it out to Swamiji which of course only gave Him an excuse to admonish His disciple teasingly,

"*Ah Badmash* (oh what a fool)! He always does these nonsense things. He must have put them like this – I didn't notice and he didn't notice either!" and all would have great fun teasing the disciple.

Once Seenu had kept Swamiji's socks stored inside His shoes, but when he went to put the shoes on Swamiji's feet, he forgot he had hidden the socks there and simply put the shoes on His feet - with the socks still inside. While out for the walk, one of the devotees pointed out to Swamiji that He was not wearing His socks today. Seenu was bewildered by it, trying to remember where he had kept the socks, but he simply couldn't remember where he had put them. It was only when they returned to the hall and Seenu removed his Guru's shoes that he found the socks inside!

Thus the day to day living with his Guru produced the usual comical errors that occur in anyone's life. A telegram arrived one day from a south Indian devotee, so Seenu, acting as Swamiji's secretary, opened the telegram and read it to Him. Now in those days telegrams were usually sent without punctuation and with as few words as possible, so as to reduce the cost, but this was often a source of vexation to the sender or the receiver as information could be easily misconstrued. Just such an incident happened this day, when Seenu read the telegram which was typed in three lines and being written in English, he translated it to Swamiji. The telegram read

' VENTAKESH LEFT
LEG NEEDS TO BE OPERATED
PRAY FOR BLESSINGS '

which in his nervous hurry, Seenu read as three separate sentences. Thus he told Swamiji in Telugu, "Oh Swamiji, Venkatesh has gone away, and now his leg needs an operation."

Swamiji appeared perplexed.

"This boy is a very nice boy - why would he go away? What will they do? Are they looking for him? Is there any other detail written there? Read it again properly and check if there are any further details there."

So Seenu checked the message again, and replied, "No

Swamiji, it simply says 'Venkatesh has left. He's gone away and his leg requires an operation.' "

Still His master was unsatisfied and continued to question Seenu about the message, feeling it did not make sense. This constant querying and replying went on for about 40 minutes with Swamiji insisting Seenu must have missed some information, and Seenu in turn feeling it was not his fault the news was bad – he was simply the messenger! After this 40 minutes of debate backwards and forwards the thought suddenly occurred to Seenu that the first two lines might be a single sentence! Feeling sheepish, wishing to bury himself in a hole in the ground, he told his Guru,

"Oh Swamiji, there is no punctuation - no full stops or apostrophe after 'Venkatesh's - it may be that Venkatesh's left leg requires an operation. Perhaps they are asking for Swamiji's blessing for the operation to be successful!"

The *Yogi* scolded him with a fond smile, "*Ah Badmash* (idiot)! You would have killed all of us with this!"

Yet for all his scolding and teasing of His disciple, Swamiji's love was more evident than His admonishment; his scoldings were not random or belligerent but were simply His careful work of moulding His masterpiece. Once or twice when Swamij was staying at the ashram, though Seenu found the work of serving Swamiji and the devotees a very blissful experience, the body's fatigue simply became overwhelming and Seenu took himself off to a secluded place where he could get a proper sleep. But he thus overslept and was not ready at 3.30 as usual with Swamiji's early morning milk. His Guru waited patiently and was asking the others if they knew where his dear boy was. He was not angry, but only concerned for Seenu's welfare.

"Why has he not come? What has happened to him? Is he alright?' he enquired earnestly of all who came to the room.

Finally at 6 o'clock Seenu was discovered sleeping in a hidden corner and after being awakened he presented himself shyly before his Guru, prepared for a dressing down, but the *Yogi* affectionately

Swamiji with Seenu on Balcony of Dehra Dun ashram

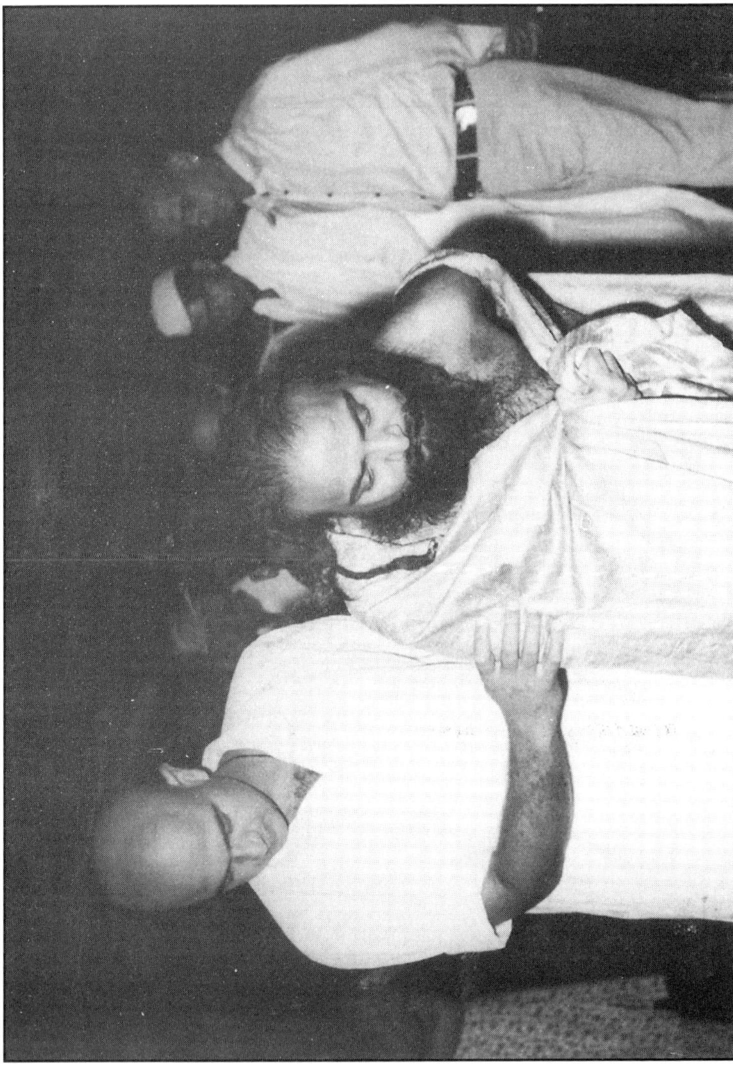

Seenu assisting Swamiji at public program

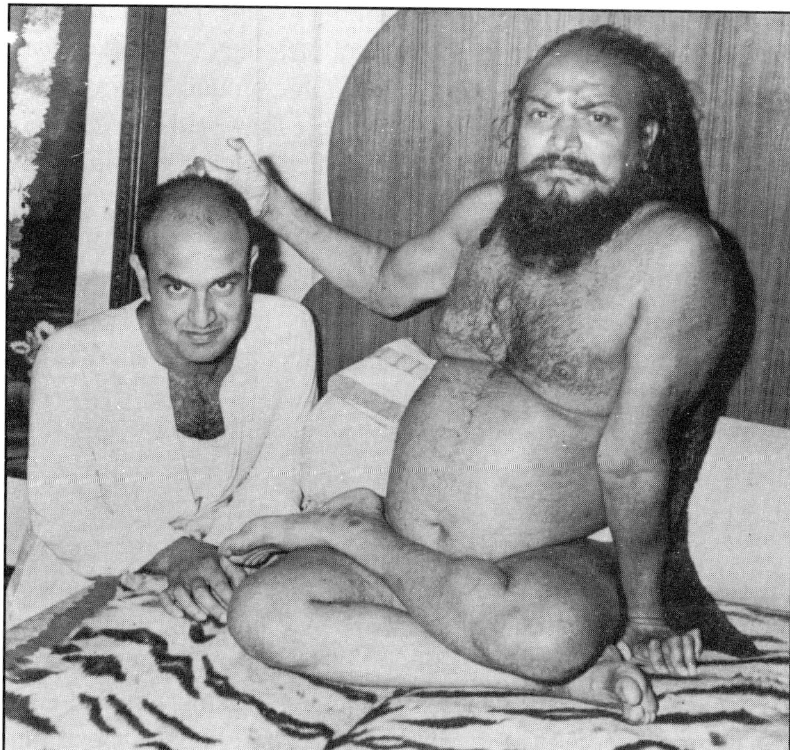

With Swamiji in Dehra Dun in 1983

assured him with all the concern of a mother, "Oh you must have been very exhausted. If you needed to sleep you could have simply told me – no need to hide like this!"

The great *Yogi* was fond of going for sea or river bathing and with the ashram situated quite close to the sacred river *Ganga* (Ganges), *Gangasnanam* (bathing in the Ganges) was a favourite way through which He gave spiritual blessings to His devotees. Secluded spots on the banks of the *Ganga* around Haridwar and Rishikesh were the favoured places where He would take devotees regularly for *Gangasnanam* through which He gave such immense bliss and spiritual blessings to so many devotees.

Once when He was staying in the Dehra Dun ashram a few devotees went with Swamiji for *Gangasnanam* and when the devotees entered the river, He noted the *poonal* (sacred thread worn by the *Brahmin* priest caste) on Seenu's body and became furious. He started yelling at his disciple,

"Why are you having this thread? It will simply give you an ego that you belong to a higher caste, which is not at all proper on the spiritual path."

Swamiji had often said that He was a "son of Mother *Ganga*", so He told Seenu to offer the sacred thread to Mother *Ganga*. Following his Guru's instructions Seenu removed the thread from his body and immersed it gently into flowing waters of the sacred river. Next Swamiji came to him and in a baptizing way sprinkled a handful of sacred *Ganga* water on Seenu's head, slapped him lovingly on the back, declaring,

"From now, remember you are a *sannyasi* (monk). But you must live a simple life so that people themselves can call you a monk, but you yourself should not become egoistic by claiming or boasting of any status as such."

In this quiet, intimate and unobtrusive manner, which so perfectly reflected their deep and personal relationship, Swamiji initiated His disciple into the holy order of *sannyas* (monkhood).

8

Yoga Vasistha and Bhava

Generally Seenu's day-to-day ashram life was peaceful and he relished the quiet, serene atmosphere and surroundings of the palatial campus. He enjoyed all the various tasks of cleaning and dusting the ashram, considering them as offerings to Swamiji who was mother, father, Guru and God for him. Behind the ashram building there was a beautiful fruit orchard and beyond that a forested area and the paddy fields of the villagers. Sometimes after his cleaning work, having bathed and performed worship at Swamiji's Shrine upstairs, he would take some *chapatis* (flat bread) that he had now learnt how to make and would retire to the orchard behind the ashram and meditate there under a majestic mango tree. His natural love of quietness and solitude found a haven there and he always found it a beautiful, peaceful and serene experience.

In 1976 Swamiji came to Dehra Dun and stayed at His ashram for about a month. During His sojourn there, in talking to Seenu one day He spoke about the spiritual text Yoga Vasistha.

"If you read and understand this book, you will find it contains the philosophy I want to convey. There would then be no need for any other scriptures. It is all about the mind and its imaginations."

After Swamiji left, a devotee brought a copy of Yoga Vasistha to the ashram, written in Hindi and compiled in two large volumes. As Seenu slowly but thoroughly devoured the text he found it became more and more revealing and interesting in its exposition of the mind and its illusory imaginations. Indeed he found he felt very peaceful after reading Yoga Vasistha.

A work of great length, Yoga Vasistha begins with the story of Lord Rama returning from a tour of his father's empire during which he has seen the day-to-day experiences of the citizens up close for the first time. His mind is unsettled and he expresses his detachment to the world and his doubts about the purpose of life, birth and death. Just at that time, sage Vishwamitra comes to the court in Ayodhya requesting of Emperor Dasaratha that he send his two children Rama and Lakshmana to safeguard his fire sacrifice from the troubling disturbance of demons, so that he can complete the ritual unhindered. At first Emperor Dasaratha refuses to send them as he feels they are too young to face such demons and instead offers that he and his army will go in their place. But sage Vishwamitra declines this offer and is interested only in taking the two young princes. Then sage Vasistha, who is also present at the court, advises the emperor to send the young men, counselling him that he should not underestimate the capabilities of Vishwamitra and of the young boys, Rama and Lakshmana.

Though still reluctant, but following the sages' advice, Dasaratha agrees to send them but then reveals that he has other concerns.

"I can definitely send them, but ever since they came back from their *yatra* (pilgrimage), Rama is totally withdrawn, remains aloof and does not talk to others, eat, smile or play. I'm very worried as Rama is to be made crown prince very soon."

Hearing this, Vasistha directs the king, "Send word to them that they should come here to the court so that I can talk to Rama and find out what his problem is."

When Rama and Lakshmana answer the summons to the court, after paying respects to the sages and elders, they sit down and Vasistha enquires of Rama why he appears suddenly so aloof and disinterested in the world around him. In response to this Rama expresses all the doubts that have started to assail him - about the purpose of life and the world's suffering, about birth and death. Sage Vasistha's reply to these queries forms the text of the great spiritual treatise we call Yoga Vasistha.

Through numerous stories, Vasistha explains how time and space are imaginations of the mind. He explains the need to control the mind and that all its imaginations and cravings are the basic reasons for the ignorance, unhappiness and fear that one experiences in the world. The dialogue carries on for seven days, and at the end of the discourse Sri Rama attains *Nirvikalpa Samadhi* and realizes the Self. This book thus gave Seenu a clear picture of what needs to be achieved and what needs to be tackled - that our own imaginations are the basic problem, and the cause of the ignorance, suffering and bondage that we create for ourselves. Having read the text it became quite clear to Seenu why Swamiji emphasized so much in His comments on meditation, mind control and the need of *sadhana* (one's efforts to achieve mind control).

During the same visit that year when Swamiji was in attendance at the ashram, in the course of the *bhajans*, a lady who was present went into a trance and starting shouting. Swamiji spoke affectionately to her and asked what she wanted. She went on demanding, "Give me something".

Laughing and joking, the *Yogi* replied, "I can give you *rothis* (bread), rice, milk or other foods - these items are possible."

Finally the lady drank a glass of milk and then, satisfied, became settled and normal as if she was released from a spell. Later the young Seenu asked Swamiji what this was all about, as he did not understand what had transpired.

Swamiji smiled warmly and told him, "Hey, don't worry. Did you get panicked at her shoutings? This is just nothing. When people go into *bhava* (trance) they get to see a vision of their *Ishta Devata* (favourite deity) and others watching them may simply see some movement in their body, based on the temperament of that individual."

Seenu asked, "Can one get Self-Realization by the trance itself or is it necessary to undertake meditation?"

"No, no", his Guru replied, "Simply going into this trance cannot give you *atma satshatkaram* (experience of the real Self).

It can be helpful in some physical ailments and assists in inducing *bhakti bhava* (strong emotional feeling of the mind) which will help one's mind to go introverted and then eventually the people may take up meditation itself more easily. Some people thus receive My blessings through trance and get encouraged to take up meditation."

Swamiji went on to explain how the use of *bhava* first started in His Mission.

In the early years, just after completing His *tapas* of 12 years when Swamiji was staying in the Adivarapupeta ashram, some devotees were sitting with Him, and Swamiji told them,

"Everything happens due to the Grace of God."

Then one of those present asked, "Whenever we want to eat, we eat. When we want to sleep, we sleep. When we want to go, we go. So where is God's Grace?"

In reply Swamiji scolded him, "Remember you cannot eat whenever you want. First you want to eat only when hungry - when you are not hungry, even if you want to eat, you cannot eat. Then even if you want to eat, if you don't get the food that you want, you cannot eat. Sometimes even if you get the food you want, if you cannot digest it, you cannot eat."

After recounting this to Seenu, Swamiji gave a roaring laugh. Continuing His story the *Yogi* related how he then instructed the devotees present to sing *bhajans*, while He Himself went into deep *dhyana samadhi*[26]. At that time some of those nearby went into a trance and started dancing and could not control their body movements. After some time Swamiji came out of *samadhi* and stopped the *kirtan* (devotional singing). Then by touching each of them between the eyebrows with His finger, these devotees were released from the trance and prostrated before Swamiji, agreeing that there is a higher power called God and that we cannot do things simply as we want.

---

[26] *Dhyana Samadhi* - A state in which a *Yogi* withdraws His mind completely back into the Self. See Glossary - 'Dhyana' and 'Samadhi'.

Then Swamiji continued, "That's why I thought of blessing people for this trance." All through this description, He was using the term '*bhava samadhi*' for 'trance'.

He explained, "Suppose you love Guru or any form of God. During this *bhava samadhi*, all your *bhava* (the mind's emotional feelings) will get concentrated on the form of your favourite deity and thus your mind becomes more concentrated, more single-pointed. Then meditation itself becomes much easier and consequently one would take up meditation more willingly. Sometimes some people do become violent and they will have to be controlled. Sometimes if some people in a trance try to be mischievous, they will be controlled by others who are in a true trance."

Thus ended the conversation for the day.

As with many things in this world wherever a genuine article exists, there is also a poor copy made. So it sometimes happened with *bhava*. There was a boy at the ashram who from time to time would pretend to be in *bhava* and often in this state would turn violent, trying to break things. At such times Swamiji Himself used to appear irritated and would ask His disciples to control him. Very often the boy would fall on Seenu during *bhajans* and try to drag the harmonium out of his hands. Seenu wondered how to deal with him, as the boy had some other devotees' support in this '*bhava*'. One day during *bhajans* when Swamiji was also there, this boy simply came running and shouting, and fell on Seenu and tore Seenu's vest. He turned very violent and was trying to drag the harmonium from his grasp and was not allowing him to sing peacefully. Instantly Seenu felt inspired to teach him a lesson. Closing his eyes as though he was also in a trance, Seenu also started shouting and fell on that boy, catching him in his arms and pinching his stomach with his fingers so that the boy fell down. One devotee who was a supporter of that boy, came shouting and declaring that the boy was in a trance but Seenu was not. After some time with all this going on, the boy stopped his disturbance.

Whatever the others may have thought, from that day onwards though he kept going into 'trance' sometimes, that boy never came near Seenu to disturb his *bhajans* again, and Seenu had his peace.

On another occasion, a large number of devotees went to nearby Rishikesh with Swamiji. It was a full moon day and night-long *kirtan* had been organized on the banks of the river *Ganga* (Ganges). There was a girl from the village across the river who used to go into 'trance' and declare that she was a goddess and that only her family members should sing during the *kirtan*. When others in the group of devotees tried to sing she would throw sand on them and so disturb them and frighten them away. On seeing this from a distance, Seenu was feeling sad and irritated, and was wondering how to deal with this girl. At this time she had closed her eyes while throwing sand around, but as she had closed her eyes she lost her sense of direction and perhaps unknown to her, came close to Swamiji - near where He was sitting. Seenu suddenly looked at Swamiji and could see annoyance in His eyes and so approached Him and asked Swamiji's permission to control her. Swamiji agreed, saying, "OK. Go and catch her and bring her here." Now half-closing his eyes, Seenu also started shouting loudly and people there thought him to be in a trance also. Seenu came near the girl and catching hold of her hair, brought her to Swamiji. Her family members started calling out, "Oh, our daughter will die. Our daughter will die."

Swamiji called them and scoldingly declared, "When your daughter was throwing sand on everyone, she was a goddess. When I gave trance to my boy to control her, suddenly you remembered that she is your daughter. If at all she was the goddess, then also you must keep quiet, because we were trying to control the goddess," and then roared with laughter.

At another time, one lady went into a false trance when they were at a temple and pretended to be possessed by the deity, demanding, "All the people at the temple with Swamiji must come and prostrate to me." The devotees became confused and some people simply went away. Seenu was certainly not impressed. He kept quiet for some time, but then she came towards him and demanded that he prostrate to her and said, "Otherwise you will be cursed and your home will be burnt." Seenu was totally clear in his mind and without any confusion, peacefully told her, "I really don't have a home that you can burn. Maybe it's best that you first give me a home and then you can think of burning it." At this, the lady then went away.

" *I have never been against* bhava samadhi *and will never be. Because true* bhava samadhi *is a great spiritual blessing that my beloved Guru Shivabalayogi bestowed upon genuine devotees to encourage them eventually to go towards meditation. I was hurt only when some people tried to abuse the name of* bhava samadhi *by behaving badly and making it appear as rubbish.*

Very often people have misunderstood me, saying that I am against bhava samadhi, *which is not correct. I have seen people going into genuine* bhava samadhi *during kirtan - in fact all such devotees who love Shivabalayogi as our beloved Guru and Father are always in one type of* bhava *(single-pointed emotions of love for the Guru) or other. Otherwise they would not be able to love the Guru as Beloved.*"

In 1977 Seenu had a chance to travel with Swamiji on His train journey to visit the royal family of Patna, in Balangir. They first travelled from Bangalore to Madras by train and then after staying there in transit for a few hours they embarked on a second train to carry on to the north. On the way, a gentleman who was travelling in the coach came to prostrate at Swamiji's Feet and was asking for information about Swamiji's life. He mentioned another *Yogi* who was in *tapas* in a village on the other bank of the river Godavari, who gave *darshan* only once a year during Mahashivaratri (annual celebration night dedicated to Lord Shiva) and for the rest of the year nobody was allowed to see him. The gentleman asked Swamiji, "Why is it that this *Yogi* has not come out of *tapas* though he commenced His *tapas* two or three years earlier than Swamiji Himself?"

To this Swamiji answered, "Before Tapaswiji Maharaj[27] came to meet Me in the early 1950's he also went to that village on the other bank of the river Godavari, but the committee there was disrespectful to the great sage and did not allow him to meet the *Balayogi* (young Yogi). Otherwise Tapaswiji Maharaj would have rightly advised that *Balayogi* with some finer points by which he could have completed the *tapas* and come out. Whereas when Tapaswiji Maharaj came to meet Me in Adivarapupeta, the keys to the *tapasmandir* (building where Swamiji sat for His *tapas*) were with My mother and she immediately took Tapaswiji Maharaj to meet Me, which was the proper way to treat such a saint. Though I was in *samadhi* when the sage paid his first visit, when he returned later for several other visits I was in waking consciousness to receive his advice about *tapas*. Tapaswiji Maharaj also advised Me to take adequate care of My physical body so as to maintain it properly."

To this the gentleman asked Him, "Swamiji, why don't you go to that village and advise that *Balayogi* to finish the *tapas* and come out?"

The *Yogi* answered, "If the committee who are looking after him write and allow me to meet him I can definitely talk to him. But the committee is arrogant."

Hearing this firm rebuff, the gentleman became quiet and didn't ask any further questions.

During the same train journey another Telugu man who was also travelling in the train from Madras would come to Swamiji every time the train stopped at a station and request that he be allowed to give something to Swamiji to eat or drink - in India it is

---

[27] *Tapaswiji Maharaj* - Tapaswiji Maharaj was a saint who gave Swamiji some advice during His *tapas* as to how to carry it through properly, and was the first to declare Swamiji as one of the greatest spiritual souls.

seen as a great privilege to be able to offer such items to Great Souls.

Swamiji was playfully funny and asked Seenu to tell that fellow that He was from the Himalayas and did not speak Telugu (though it was in fact His mother tongue) and did not know any other language other than a little bit of Hindi. To enliven the drama Swamiji made some funny sign language which the man could not understand. Finally when the train stopped in Bobilli, Andra Pradesh, Swamiji finally told Seenu in Hindi that when that person came again to ask him to bring a tender coconut which would have the coconut water inside. So Seenu did as instructed and when the fellow brought the tender coconut, he also brought a knife so that Seenu could pierce the coconut and drain out the coconut water inside.

" Then Swamiji asked me to pierce the coconut with the knife and pour that coconut water into His glass. Any time Swamiji gave me some work, he would always tease me and make me nervous so I would end up doing some funny things. I pierced the coconut and holding the glass in one hand, with the coconut in the other, I tilted the coconut to pour the water into the glass. However as I was pouring the coconut water, Swamiji suddenly shouted in Hindi,

'Hey idiot, careful, careful. You will spill the coconut water on the ground!'

I thus became nervous and tilted that coconut over to pour out the water, but then also tilted the glass in my other hand upside down as well and spilt all the coconut water on the ground. I immediately became panicked that Swamiji would start yelling and shouting at me but He simply started laughing and with a roaring voice declared,

'I know this idiot - he would definitely do this.'

By then the train started moving so that man who had brought the coconut simply went away. For a long time Swamiji always teased me by telling this story to other devotees and calling me, 'Paramandaya Sishya' [28]. "

On another journey Swamiji and some accompanying devotees including Seenu, went to visit Ananthapur where Swamiji had another ashram. The group was planning to leave at 4.00am for a six to seven hour journey, but around 10.30pm on the previous evening, suddenly Swamiji said they would leave immediately for Ananthapur. All were promptly informed and they left at about 11.00pm. After a few hours' journey, Swamiji abruptly ordered that the car be stopped and got out of the car and started walking around it for some time. The devotees were wondering why Swamiji had stopped the car and was walking here and there in the middle of the night for no apparent reason. After about half an hour, as suddenly as He had stopped, He got back into the car and declared, "Now we can move."

After travelling for about a further 45 minutes, suddenly coming into the view of the headlights they saw, lying on the road, some people who had been attacked and injured. Some bandits had waylaid them and assaulted them severely - one man was bleeding profusely.

Swamiji said, "Look if we had come straight away without stopping, we would have got involved with the robbers."

He applied some blessed *vibhuti* to the man who was bleeding and by then they flagged down another car which was passing on the same road and with the assistance of those travellers, transported the injured man to the hospital and informed the local police.

" *Thus unknown to us Swamiji had saved all of us from the* dacoits *(robbers). Later we reached Ananthapur much earlier than scheduled, and after a beautiful program there, returned the same night to Bangalore.*"

---

[28] *Paramandaya Sishya* - 'Paramandaya's disciple'. Paramandaya was a legendary Guru whose stories are quite familiar in Andra Pradesh where Swamiji grew up. Stories about Him often refer to His disciples' comic or silly behaviour and one well-known story is similar to this incident, with a disciple spilling a drink through his confusion.

9

In the Guru's Service

In 1978 when Swamiji visited Dehra Dun during the summer months He spoke to Seenu about a mentally retarded boy in Mysore, whose brothers Seenu had known when he lived there before entering the ashram's service. The boy was violent at home, such that the family kept him locked in a room without even shaving him as he would attack members of the family if they approached him and thus the family members were scared to go near or handle him too much. Years before, Swamiji had told the family that if the boy came to the ashram he would be alright.

Swamiji told Seenu, "If you are interested to look after him I will send him here", and then in the same breath continued, "I'll tell you a story about what happens when one listens to the Guru's words."

" In the olden days the Gurus used to go trekking from place to place followed by their disciples and at the end of each day they would camp on the outskirts of the nearest village. After bathing in the river, the disciples would go into the village to beg for *bhiksanam* (alms), bring the collected food, offer it to the Guru for His blessing and then all would share it. Once one Guru went on walking for a long distance for several days without stopping anywhere. It was a test for the disciples and though they became very hungry, they would not dare ask for any food until the Guru Himself directed them. Eventually after six or seven days of this journeying they were walking in the forest and they came across a dead dog's body which was decaying and emitting a foul smell. The smell was repulsive. Seeing the dead dog's body thus, the Guru said teasingly,

'Oh, poor children you must be very hungry, so all of you can eat this dog.'

The disciples were disgusted at the site of the dead dog and stayed away, saying, 'Oh, such a foul smell. We cannot eat it.'

But one of the disciples thought, 'Because Guruji has ordered this, there must be some reason. So let me eat the dog,' and as he went closer and put his hands out to eat it, the dog's decayed body was miraculously converted into beautiful sweets and he ate them very happily. Now the other disciples felt ashamed and murmured amongst themselves,

'Look, we did a foolish thing. We should have trusted the Guru's words without questioning. Because this boy listened he got to eat the sweets. Next time whenever the Guru orders us to do anything, without questioning we will carry it out.'

So the Guru and his band went on travelling again for several days and finally the group came to the outskirts of a village. Sitting there the Guru instructed them, 'There is a ghost in that banyan tree. It is waiting for my *darshan*. If you can catch it and bring it here I can bless the ghost and it will be liberated from its tortured state.'

Although all the disciples were hungry and tired, they thought, 'This time let us do as the Guru has ordered. Maybe we will get some sort of reward by following His command.'

Thus competing with each other one by one they went to bring that ghost to their Guru. But as they approach it, they were all beaten and driven away by the spectre. Disappointed, they all returned grumbling and complaining to their Guru that they were beaten and injured in their attempts to catch hold of the ghost. But the same disciple who had eaten the decayed dog's body which became sweets, first came and prostrated at the Lotus Feet of the Guru and prayed to Him thus, 'Dear Guru, please bless me. Give me a trick so that I can bring the ghost to You.'

Pleased, the Guru instructed him, 'Quietly go to the ghost and keep talking in a very friendly way and when you get close enough suddenly catch hold of its hair. Then you will be able to bring the ghost here to Me.'

So the disciple did as directed by the Guru and approached the ghost speaking nicely to it until he came close enough to grasp its hair, and then suddenly grabbing its tresses, he led the ghost to the Guru for His *darshan*. By the grace of the Guru, the ghost was liberated.

The Guru ridiculed the other disciples, 'As you have to carry out My orders, if you do not understand anything you must ask and pray to the Guru for proper instructions and advice. When you went to perform this task you had the motive of trying to gain some worldly benefit from Me; you did not really have faith in the Guru and the Guru's words - this is why you didn't succeed.' "

After telling this story Swamiji gave a thunderous laugh and told Seenu, "If you say that you can look after that boy, I will send him here."

In reply Seenu said that he would like to look after the boy as wanted by Swamiji.

"I pray that Swamiji please bless me so that the boy will not be violent here and will listen to me."

Smiling warmly Swamiji answered, "Look, all you have to do is - love him. When he becomes adamant, just threaten that you will send him back to Mysore; then he'll be alright."

So the mentally retarded boy came to stay with Seenu in the ashram and while initially he did give some trouble, gradually under Seenu's kind but firm hand he started listening to instructions and Seenu taught him to perform various duties around the ashram grounds such as watering the plants and locking the gates and doors of the ashram. Seenu shaved his face and gradually tried to teach him more complex tasks such as washing his own clothes and having a bath. He taught the boy to pump the bellows of the harmonium to carry on a particular set *shruti* (note) and with the boy carrying this on continually, Seenu would sing the *bhajans* while himself playing the *dholak*. Like this, every evening for an hour Seenu and the boy performed their *sadhana* and finished with *arathi* (ceremonial salute with light) - often the boy would continue dedicatedly playing the *shruti* even after the singing was finished and would only stop when Seenu directed him to. Thus he became very attached to Seenu and the disciple spent 13 long years looking after the boy - like a mother would a child - as a service to his beloved Guru, Sri Swamiji.

Finally the boy became sick with renal failure, and until the last moment Seenu nursed him lovingly and tried to give some spiritual solace to his mind. But the boy's health deteriorated and in the last few days of his life Seenu stayed with him, singing bhajans and praying for the Divine Grace to be showered on the soul, trying to make his death as non-violent as possible. In November 1991, on the boy's last day on this earth Seenu was singing *Lingashtakam* (song in praise of Shivalingam) and keeping a hand on the boy's heart, and gently poured some sacred Ganges water[29] into his mouth just before he breathed his last.

Other than this, some devotees whose children were boarding in a local public school wanted Seenu to look after their children as a local guardian, with Swamiji's permission. Seenu's job was to take them for an outing on Sundays, give them food, perhaps enjoy an excursion of some sort and then drop them back at school. This went on for many years. Though it was unusual work for a monk, Seenu always simply considered it as service to his Guru.

" *One day when I was bathing Him, Swamiji suddenly asked, 'Hey ,do you think that you came to do meditation but instead you have a lot of odd jobs in this ashram life? Do not consider that you are being given odd jobs to do. Have faith in the name of*

---

[29] Ganges water - The river Ganges is considered by Indians to be the most sacred river. It is an Indian tradition to drink the water from the sacred river Ganges just before dying, to help clear the mind of its impressions.

Guru. With total devotion consider everything as a service to the Guru and His Mission. Then every karma *(action) of yours will get converted into* sadhana. *Often Swamiji mentioned the word* 'sadhana' *and emphasized the need to undertake* sadhana. *Generally* sadhana *means 'your efforts to achieve something'.*

Swamiji explained the term as, 'Simply your work to achieve mind control.'

He used to say, 'If you surrender mentally to the Guru through service, then automatically your mind gets controlled.' At one public darshan *session a person once complained about having lost peace of mind and Swamiji asked him, 'Do you do some* sadhana*?' As Swamiji spoke mainly in Telugu I needed to translate what He said into Hindi for the man and I translated it as, 'Are you practicing any meditation?'*

Swamiji pulled me up and corrected me, 'When I said "sadhana"*, why are you using the word "meditation"? Meditation means that a person will be sitting and closing the eyes. But* "sadhana" *can happen during* Dhyana *(meditation), through* Bhakti *(devotion), through* Seva *(service) and in so many ways when one is able to surrender to the Guru. If you surrender to the Guru, automatically the mind will get controlled.'*

So thus Swamiji always emphasized 'Do sadhana. *Do* sadhana'. *Through this one word* 'sadhana', *Swamiji beautifully conveyed the essence of the whole message that the Bhagavad Gita contains.' "*

Later that year when Swamiji was returning to Bangalore, he took Seenu with Him. Though he didn't want Seenu to go to any other relative, he was always happy to send him to visit his mother; she was a great source of inner strength for him. She wrote to Seenu in the ashram regularly every week and did not demand any reply immediately, knowing he was busy. She always used to write, "Be more determined and be humble. Come to meet me only when Swamiji permits it. Do not demand unnecessarily." She always encouraged him to serve and keep doing *sadhana* to obtain God's and Guru's Grace. At one time, about a year after Seenu had joined the ashram when his mother came to have Swamiji's *darshan*, He blessed her, "You have donated your child to Me and so no harm will come to your family. God will always protect you all and give peace and prosperity."

When Seenu visited Bangalore, after giving the morning bath and breakfast to Swamiji he used to take His permission and go to spend a few hours with his mother before returning for the evening *meditation, bhajans* and *arathi*. Just as when He stayed in Dehra Dun, many a time late at night Swamiji would sing *bhajans* and used to ask Seenu to play the harmonium as accompaniment. For Seenu those times were the most precious, receiving Swamiji's spiritual vibrations and blessings in such an intimate setting.

During this particular visit the Bangalore ashram had purchased a table and a few chairs through an auction of items manufactured by some local prisoners. Then one evening after *arathi*, the table was placed near the entrance door of the main *bhajan mandir* (song hall).

Swamiji asked Seenu, "Where do you want to sit at the table to work - in the office, inside that room or near that entrance door?"

Now the young disciple saw some sweets in front of Swamiji on the dais and just for fun requested of his Guru, "If You give me those sweets to me, I will go and sit near the door."

" *Taking out a sweet, Swamiji gave it to me from His hand and told me, 'Look you asked for the sweets, so I am giving to you. But now you must go to the door, sit on the chair in front of the table and do not get up until I come there', to which I replied, 'OK Swamiji, I will do that.'*

Saying so, I went and sat up on the chair near the door. Usually every day after His dinner Swamiji would come out and keep walking around the hall and into the outside compound and the garden. But that day, perhaps deliberately, Swamiji did not come out after His dinner. He sent word to me through some devotees, 'Ask him to get up and go to have his food. Swamiji will not be coming out today and for a whole month He will not come out.'

But I refused to get up and said, 'I will get up only when Swamiji comes here, as He has ordered. I will be sitting here until He comes.'

He had told the kitchen boy that I should be given food only if I got up from the table and came to the kitchen, not if I stayed at the table. Some time later He sent some more devotees to tell me, 'Swamiji is very angry. He's annoyed with you that you didn't go to the kitchen to have your food. Swamiji may beat you up and throw you out of the ashram.'

But I was totally determined not to get up until Swamiji Himself came. Finally everybody went away to sleep and I was sitting alone, totally swarmed by a cloud of mosquitoes for whom it seemed to be a festival day - biting me all over my body. All the time I was repeating "Om Shivaya Shivabalayogendraya Parabrahmanaya", the mantra that Swamiji had given to me in my dream.

In the early hours of the morning, around 4 o'clock, Swamiji remembered that I might be sitting there quietly and came with a torchlight. In delight at His coming, I prostrated to my Guru for His blessings. Then I prayed to Swamiji to sit on the chair and did arathi *to Him.*

Pleased, Swamiji asked the kitchen boy to give me my food.

He said, 'This was a test for you and you have passed. When you are trying to achieve something you need to be totally determined and persevere come what may.' "

During this same visit to Bangalore, Swamiji was quite unhappy with one of His *tapaswin* (engaged in *tapas*) disciples. A boy who had been engaged in *tapas* in one of the ashrams for about 3 years, was getting disturbed and wanted to get up and cease the grueling *sadhana*. He even used to threaten the man in charge of the ashram that he would transform him into a sheep or goat if he wasn't allowed to leave. Swamiji Himself went there several times to enquire about his problems and the boy used to tell Swamiji that he was experiencing very dreaded, terrifying visions. Swamiji advised him not to worry and to proceed with determination and assured him that everything would be alright - but day by day he was getting more and more disturbed. Seenu had previously seen that boy in *tapas* during a prior visit to that town with Swamiji. The boy had exhibited a beautiful glowing aura around his face at that time and Swamiji had also said at that time that he was attaining a good *samadhi*(mind-stilled) state. Swamiji had remarked that He had asked the boy to do five years of *tapas*, but in the later part of 1978 the young man discontinued doing the *tapas* and simply went away.

Now Seenu had heard about this boy through Tilakamma when she had been with him in Dehra Dun in 1974 and the boy was engaged in the *tapas* at that point. After hearing these stories about him at that time, a desire developed within Seenu that he might himself one day perform *tapas* and every day thereafter he used to include in his daily prayers, a prayer to Swamiji to bless him that he might be able to perform *tapas* and become a *Yogi*. So when this boy did not listen to Swamiji's advice, left his *tapas* and went away, Seenu felt very disturbed that the young aspirant had not listened to the Guru's advice and had missed such a rare opportunity in this universe, to realize the Self - but still Seenu's desire to do *tapas* remained.

During this stay in Bangalore in 1978, in September it was Seenu's birthday and on the previous evening someone had given him a milk chocolate as a present. On the morning of his birthday at 4 o'clock, after having his bath he went to Swamiji's room to convey that it was his birthday and pray for His blessing by prostrating at His Lotus Feet. Swamiji was very kind and affectionate when Seenu presented the chocolate to Him as an offering. The *Yogi* bit off half the chocolate and returned the other half to Seenu urging him to eat it as *prasadam* immediately.

Swamiji told him, "Eating *prasadam* has great significance. One should eat the *prasadam* then and there itself. Tapaswiji Maharaj once told Me about one devotee who took the gift of *prasad* very casually and kept it aside thinking that he would eat it the next day - but before the next day came, he died overnight. That's why one should never delay eating *prasad*."

Emboldened by the day being his birthday, Seenu felt moved to ask his Guru to initiate him into *tapas*. Taking a piece of *vibhuti*, he offered it to His Guru, asking Swamiji to bless it.

" *Swamiji asked, 'Why do you want this* vibhuti*?'*

Spontaneously it come out of my mouth, 'I want to do tapas. *I want to sit and do* tapas.*'*

Jokingly perhaps, Swamiji asked me, 'Do you think this vibhuti *can make you to sit for* tapas*?'*

'Swamiji, I have faith. If You please bless this vibhuti *I am sure the* vibhuti *can definitely make me do* tapas. *If You bless it, it can definitely happen.'*

Then Swamiji smiled. He blessed the vibhuti *and gave it to me. But He said, 'Faith in the name of Guru can work wonders. If you want to sit for* tapas *now, I can make you sit for* tapas*; but if you sit for* tapas *now, instead of successfully completing it you might acquire some ego and you may even go away from me physically and may not be able to serve in My Mission.'*

I replied, 'Swamiji, then I do not want to do tapas. *Because what I want is Swamiji, that's all I know. I love You and I want to be in Swamiji's Mission. I want to serve You only. Whether I get Realized or not - that is not so important for me - but definitely I would like to remain at Your Lotus Feet and serve You forever.*

" Then Swamiji smiled. ' Take this vibhuti' *and keep it with you. In due course of time when the time is ripe, you will get what you want.*"

The daily routine continued and as usual included a generous amount of scolding. Whenever Swamiji would get annoyed with Seenu and shout at him - often for a long time - Seenu felt that it was a blessing and was done to make him stronger and test his determination.

Swamiji would tell him, "Just like you require physical stamina to run a marathon, in the same way you require mental stamina for your life on this earth and to achieve your target, for it is always a long battle." After scolding him, He used to tease Seenu, "Now that I have scolded you, your mind might want to run away from Me but you need to have the faith that Lord Hanuman had in his Guru, Sri Rama. If you have that faith even the Guru cannot harm you and will have to shower His blessings. If you take the Guru's name, it is always powerful for you."

" So many times He told us this story. He used to repeat the stories so many times to make them penetrate into our minds and hearts.

He used to recount, "Hanuman's mother had told him, 'Whoever can recognize your earrings is your Lord Guru. Do not give up taking His name and serving Him till the last breath of your life.'

Finally when Sri Rama and Lakshmana were going in search of Sita they came to the region of the monkey kingdom. Hanuman came as a spy disguised as a Brahmin priest on the order of his king Sugriva, to check over Rama and Lakshmana as to who they were. At first Lakshmana was apprehensive about the intentions of this priest, but Sri Rama said, 'Look at his glowing face and his beautiful earrings. He cannot be a demon. He must be a great noble soul.' When Hanuman heard this, he remembered his mothers words and decided, 'Oh this must be my real Master and Lord', and leapt with excitement and totally surrendered to Lord Rama in the bhava *(attitude) of a servant.*

Then when Sri Rama had returned to Ayodhya after killing the demon king Ravana and was ruling over the empire, there was once a big conference in Devaloka (the world of gods) in which all the angels, gods and great sages were participating and the matter of the discussion turned toward the topic, 'Which one is more powerful - Sri Rama's bow and arrows, or Sri Rama's name?'

The venerable sage Vishwamitra declared, 'I have no doubt in saying that Lord Rama's bows and arrows are more powerful than anything else. Even today if Sri Rama stands with his bows and arrows, nobody in the universe can challenge him.'

To this sage Vasistha declared, 'No, I have a different opinion. Sri Rama's name is much more powerful than Sri Rama's bows and arrows. I can definitely say that whoever is devoted to Sri Rama's name and takes Sri Rama's name with total faith and devotion, even Sri Rama himself cannot harm such a person with his bows and arrows.'

At this rebuke, sage Vishwamitra was furious and declared, 'Then we will test this to prove it one way or the other.'

Coming down from Devaloka to the empire of Ayodhya, Vishwamitra went to a kingdom within the empire where the ruling king was very devoted to Lord Rama. Vishwamitra deliberately went to the palace when that king was deep in meditation and because of this could not attend to the proper reception of Vishwamitra and welcome him as was the normal protocol (always in India, sages were welcomed and offered reception by washing their feet and giving them a respectable seat and the host would properly enquire after their welfare).

Taking this as an excuse, Vishwamitra then went to the court of Lord Rama and complained,

'Within your empire, a king has been disrespectful to me by not welcoming me to his court properly. Now I don't want to stay in your empire and I will go away somewhere else.'

Lord Rama begged Vishwamitra's pardon and requested the sage to tell him who it was that had been so disrespectful. In the same breath Lord Rama took a terrible vow, 'I take a vow in the name of my bows and arrows through which I killed the great demon kings like Ravana and Kumbhakarna, that before sunset tomorrow I will cut off the head of this person who has been disrespectful to you, sage Vishwamitra.'

Now sage Narada who was always fond of watching the divine play, had also been at the conference in Devaloka. So he came to the kingdom where the king unknowingly upset Vishwamitra and warned the king that his own Lord Rama had vowed to punish him by cutting off his head before the next day's sunset. Being a devotee of Lord Rama, the king was unconcerned at this threat to his life but Narada explained that this was a test of the power of Lord Rama's name and that he must act out his part in the drama by trying to avoid death.

The sage advised him, 'Look if at all anybody can protect you, it is Lord Hanuman who is a disciple of Lord Rama and always keeps reciting Rama's name, whether simply sitting on a treetop or on the top of a mountain - everywhere he goes. First go and surrender to Lord Hanuman and beg for his protection without letting on who is going to kill you. As Sri Hanuman is fond of Lord Rama's devotees, get him to promise that he will protect you and only then should you tell him that Sri Rama is the one who is going to kill you.'

So the king went to Sri Hanuman and told him what was going to happen to him the next day and begged for his protection. As Hanuman was coming out of a samadhi *(stillness of the mind) state, in the same breath Hanuman declared, 'Do not worry oh king. I promise you in Lord Rama's name, which is dearer to me all day and night, that no power can harm your life!' After extracting this promise, the king then informed Hanuman that it was Sri Rama who had vowed to kill him.*

To this Hanuman declared, 'Oh God! You will make me fight with my Guru!' but then he thought, 'Maybe this is a divine play.' So, thinking what to do, he built a fort out of his own tail and made the king sit inside there safely.

The next day Lord Rama sent his armies and all his brothers to find the king and kill him. When they could not succeed because

Hanuman was protecting him, finally Lord Rama himself came and ordered his disciple to hand over the king, telling him that he had promised sage Vishwamitra that he would kill the king and had taken a vow in the name of his bows and arrows.

At this Sri Hanuman prostrated before his Guru and stood with folded hands, 'My Lord, mentally I surrender to You and say that when You would drop Your physical body, the power of Your bows and arrows will also vanish and will be of no use to humanity in the coming ages. But the mantra of my Lord Rama's name will be the most useful mantra for humanity in the coming ages. Even after You are no longer on this earth physically, it is Your name by taking which the people of this world can attain Bhakti *(devotion) and* Moksha *(liberation). So I cannot allow my Lord Rama's name to prove false.'*

Thus Hanuman stood with folded hands and refused to hand over the king, but simply kept reciting Sri Rama's name with total faith and devotion. All the sages and angels had gathered to see this divine play and anxiously they wondered, 'What is going to happen next?'

Sri Rama roared, 'Well then first I will kill you, Hanuman, and then this king', and started shooting arrows with lightning speed, one after another. To the amazement of all those who had gathered there, as they flew through the sky, all the arrows transformed into flower garlands and fell gently around Hanuman's neck.

Telling this story so many times to me, Swamiji would say, 'Look at the power of faith and devotion in the name of Guru. If you have faith in your Guru, even the Guru cannot hurt you.'

He also used to say, 'Never should one betray the Guru and give up the Guru. One should always be devoted with total faith to the Guru till the last breath of life.' "

Once when speaking about Faith and Service with some devotees, suddenly Swamiji looked over at Seenu, saying to all those present, "Look at the faith and attachment that Seenu has. Even if I cut him into pieces and throw him in the river, he will get joined back together and come back to me."

10

Mission Work

In the following year when Swamiji was in residence at His Dehra Dun ashram, one of His devotees who had come with Him from Bangalore and was very attached to Swamiji, always serving Him with total faith and devotion, went to a nearby ashram and met the resident monk there. This devotee firmly believed that Swamiji was the incarnation of so many great saints, as mentioned in the *Nadis*[30]. He therefore declared to the ashram monk, "My Guru Shivabalayogi was born as your Guru in His previous incarnation. Why don't you come and meet Him?"

Now that monk did not like the idea and politely asked him to leave the place. So the devotee then returned to Swamiji's ashram depressed, and came and lamented in front of the *Yogi*,

"Swamiji, these monks don't want to believe that You were their Guru in Your previous incarnation."

Swamiji became furious and scolded that devotee, "Idiot. Who told you to go there and claim that I was their Guru in a previous incarnation? If you have that belief, keep it to yourself - no need to advertise in a big way. I had to do 12 years of *tapas* to become Shivabalayogi and there is no need for me to claim that I was another Guru in my previous incarnation and there is no need for me to create any controversy to become famous."

---

[30] *Nadis* - The Nadis are astrological readings, said to be of a person's previous incarnations. Readings of the Nadis pertaining to Swamiji declared Him to be have been born previously as so many Great Souls, well-known throughout India.

Then Swamiji spoke about one saint who first claimed to be the incarnation of another famous saint and thus unnecessarily created controversy for a mere publicity stunt, to become famous in that way. He then suddenly turned to Seenu and asked,

"Hey Seenu, tomorrow when I drop my physical body and somebody else comes and claims that he is Shivabalayogi, would you allow him to stay in my room or sit on the dais that I'm sitting on today?"

Without any confusion Seenu replied, "I can honour any other saint if they come, but can never accept anybody else even if it is God, as my beloved Guru Shivabalayogi and would never allow such a person to stay in Swamiji's room or sit on Swamiji's dais as long as I am alive."

At this Swamiji smiled and said to the devotee, "See. That is the correct answer. Then how do you expect devotees of other Gurus to accept Me as a manifestation of their own Guru?"

Thus Swamiji never really claimed anything about Himself. Though devotees had their own faith and beliefs, Swamiji never tried to encourage or impose any one particular notion. He left it to the belief of the individual devotee. All He emphasized was to practice meditation. When once one boy asked Him, "Swamiji were you really Ramakrishna Paramahamsa in your previous life?", Swamiji laughed and said,

"When did I tell you that? If some devotees believe so, it is their belief. If they want to think so, they can think it. No problem for me."

These things Swamiji never advocated in any particular way - He simply left it to the temperament and belief of the particular devotees. Sometimes He said, "Yes", sometimes He said, "No need for that." Sometimes He remained quiet without making any answer. He might have taught different devotees in different ways. Reflecting later, Seenu recalled,

" *Somehow He tried to groom me in a particular way, perhaps according to my temperament. Though I never saw Swamiji prescribing any particular way of life to any particular devotee, He groomed me up very caringly and affectionately and always recommended that though He has not given me any saffron-coloured clothes, within my mind I should not forget that I am a* sannyasi *(monk).*"

Swamiji spoke infrequently in public and never gave long public lectures. He offered His *darshan* and the *dyhana diksha* (meditation initiation) freely but otherwise taught mainly through silence – the devotee needed to be attentive and receptive to take this in. Thus when He did speak, though the comment might be brief, it carried great import. Once a person attending one program asked Him, "Swamiji, You teach about mind control. What is mind control?"

Swamiji was sitting on the dais and there were some flowers next to Him, so picking up one of the flowers, He threw it through the air.

" *Turning to the person who had asked Him the question, He simply said, 'See if My mind goes after the flower and gets glued to it, that is the mind going out of control. If I don't allow my mind to go out of control and keep it here – that is mind control. Simple.'*

In this way He would answer queries in a very simple but complete manner – like a sutra *(scriptural aphorism).* "

During one stay in Bangalore, a young boy came and innocently asked Him, "Swamiji I want Self-Realization."

Looking at Him commandingly, the *Yogi* instructed him, "Go and buy a pair of shoes and then hit those shoes on your head strongly. Then you will get Self-Realization – go."

" *I simply interpreted it that if you can lose the ego then you will become Self-Realized.*"

Though from the outside He appeared very harsh and was all the time trying to find fault with Seenu, yelling and shouting at him, that was all for a specific purpose of training him to be mentally tough. He always used to say, "Your mind needs to be very strong to work in the Mission otherwise people will eat you up."

After scolding He would sometimes say, "Take my scoldings - then you will become so strong that this world cannot trouble you anymore."

About Himself He used to say, "Doing 12 years of *tapas* was very easy for me as I always remained in *samadhi* and never took any troubles to the mind or cared. But when I came out of *tapas* and tried to establish the Mission - my God! These people of the world - they ate my head!" In the same breath He used to say, "Well, I am not a person to care or bother for these things", and would give a thunderous laugh.

On several occasions He spoke in a discouraging way if the subject of Seenu getting married was brought up. He cared for Seenu just like a mother would care for her child. Once one of the college professors from Mysore who was a devotee of Swamiji's, had come for Swamiji's *darshan* in Bangalore.

The *Yogi* asked him, "Hey, what should I do with my boy Seenu? Should I ask him to marry or not?"

Then the professor said, "It is nice Swamiji if he can marry. Both he and his wife can look after the ashram."

Immediately Swamiji replied, "What is the guarantee that his wife will allow him to look after the ashram peacefully? She could be dragging him into other ways of life. Tell me what would you have done if you had met me at such a tender age, like Seenu met me at the age of sixteen?"

The professor answered, "Surely Swamiji I wouldn't have married and would have stayed with You only, forever."

"Then why do you want Seenu to get married now? Let him enjoy the life in the ashram with Me, unmarried."

At another time, while a group of people were giving the daily oil massage to Swamiji's body, one devotee said, "Swamiji, make Seenu marry and when he gets children You will have more devotees around." Swamiji shot back abruptly, "Did the demon king Hiranyakashipu[31] ever think that his son Prahlada would go against his father's wishes and became a devotee of Lord Vishnu? So what if Seenu's son also goes against his wishes by not becoming a devotee of Swamiji? Seenu as one devotee is enough for Me."

Then looking at Seenu tenderly Swamiji said, "Hey these people have no mind to talk. We both, Guru and *shishya* (disciple), do not require any marriage. We have plenty of other important things to do in this world. These people of the world cannot think of anything other than marriage."

On another time in Adivarapupeta, Swamiji's stepmother[32] came to see Him. Swamiji sent his nephew with Seenu to introduce him, "Just like you adopted Swamiji in His childhood, Swamiji has adopted Seenu as His son."

With any young man of marriageable age, it is common in India that their prospective marriage is the first focus of conversation when meeting them, so she asked, "Are you married? Has Swamiji looked for any girl for you?"

Swamiji was always very straightforward in His speech, and He shot back, "What happiness did you get from your marriage? Marriage means keeping a big boulder on your head. Let him be happy without marriage."

Like this, Swamiji always took very special care to keep Seenu's mind away from worldly life, though sometimes he used

---

[31] *Hiranyakashipu* - A legendary demon king who took Lord Vishnu as his enemy, but whose son Prahlada was a great devotee of Vishnu.

[32] *Swamiji's Stepmother* - Swamiji's father, Bheemana, first married Shravanamma. But because they did not have any children, with Shravanamma's permission, Bheemana took a second wife - Parvathamma (Swamiji's mother) - as is allowed in old Hindu custom. Shravanamma later adopted Sathyaraju and hence is referred to as Swamiji's stepmother.

to tease his pupil to test his mind.

Suddenly He would say, "Seenu tell me if you have any desires for marriage or any girl in your mind."

" *I always prayed and refused, as not even once had any such thoughts come into my mind. All I wanted was Swamiji. I felt very blissful watching Swamiji and sometimes I even felt irritated when Swamiji used to be talking and used to pray within my mind, 'Swamiji please can You not sit quietly. I just want to keep watching You and did not want anything else. You are my God and everything for me.'* "

Many a day when Swamiji was not staying in Dehra Dun, after finishing his morning duties of cleaning the ashram and completing the morning *puja* (worship) Seenu used to make some *chapatis* (flat bread) for himself for lunch and quietly slip into the backyard orchard and sit under a beautiful mango tree there or retire to a banyan tree in nearby forest. These were favourite places where Seenu would spend hours quietly absorbed in meditation. Yoga Vasistha gave him an insight into the real concept of meditation and what really needs to be achieved through meditation. Shortly the understanding started coming to him that the real problem is within one's own mind and that to whatever imaginations the mind becomes habituated, the world and its people will appear thus. The atmosphere in the backyard fruit orchard or the forest would be very peaceful and quiet and he always loved this type of solitude - hours would pass by quietly unnoticed by the mind. Sometimes in the late afternoon or evening hours when he would come out of the meditation he would eat the *chapatis* he had cooked in the morning before returning to the ashram to attend to the evening duties of *arathi* and *puja*.

As nobody knew he was there sometimes people might have thought he had gone to town for some work or gone to gossip somewhere. There was one man, a devotee of the ashram, who thought himself to be very close to Swamiji but he was always fond of dominating and controlling things. He used to threaten Seenu, "So many times I telephoned the ashram to see what you were doing - I never got any answer! So where were you - missing, not attending to your duties? I can always complain to Swamiji and see that you are sent away from this place."

Whenever incidents such as this happened, whether the event was a small or larger one, Seenu always tried to visualize them as a test by the Divine Guru of his determination. He simply felt pity for such people and prayed to the Divine Guru to bless them for purity of heart and better understanding and quietly went on with his *sadhana* not bothered about anybody's reaction. The man who had come from Karnataka always tried to utilize this sort of situation against Seenu so that Swamiji would get annoyed with him and perhaps send him out of the ashram, because the fellow was always unhappy with Seenu that he had told Swamiji about the '*bhang*' incident. He and the man who supplied it to him were always trying to find some excuse to put some blame or other onto the young disciple.

" *During my life in the ashram there came so many incidents which taught me such great lessons. I learnt that no path was free from obstacles, no journey complete without a challenge and in life on this earth one will always have to face the dualities of good and bad. If some were very affectionate and always caring to me, others behaved as if I was their worst enemy - it appeared as if my simple existence there was a stumbling block for them. I also learnt many amongst humans are experts in manipulating situations for their selfish interests and just giving lip service to spiritual ideals. Such people appear so sweet in front of others but when it comes to action they behave very cunningly. Though at times it hurt the sensitiveness of my mental consciousness slowly I learnt to see every such incident as a blessing in disguise, created and sent by the Divine Guru to train me to become more refined. So silently I took everything - whether good or bad - as the Divine Guru's Grace. But sometimes these things made me think, from sadness and hurt feelings rather than from anger, 'Maybe the animal world is better - perhaps human beings are the most wretched creatures of this world.'*

Sometimes when this type of people were after my life and finding some excuse to blame me for something, one really felt disgusted and I thought I must go away to places where I would not have to see any human beings at all. Once I was hurt so badly and the sadness of detachment was so strong one evening, I left the ashram and went into the nearby forest. It was the month of January with a severe winter at its peak and the next day was my beloved Swamiji's birthday celebrations. I had spent the whole night shivering in the cold, quietly trying to remember my beloved Guru Swamiji. I had gone away from the ashram because the pressure tactics and trouble became so unbearable for the sensitiveness of my mental consciousness. After nearly 24 hours, my mind slowly started getting pulled by the remembrance of my beloved Guru and the trauma in the mind receded considerably. Then wisdom thoughts came and I remembered the promises made to my mother that I would not go away from the Guru or the ashram on my own, unless sent out by the Guru Himself.

So the thoughts continued, 'Why should I bother about what others are thinking of me? Let them complain to Swamiji. Until and unless Swamiji Himself asks me to go away, why should I go away from the ashram?' "

So straight away he came back to the ashram. He could also see that his mind was totally attached to Swamiji and it was so unbearably painful to stay away from Him or the ashram. He thought, "Without His name, without serving Him or His Mission, my life has no meaning." But when he returned to the ashram, the man from Karnataka was not ready to open the door and allow him inside. The man was furious and perhaps may have thought that this was a good opportunity to drive Seenu away. But Swamiji's nephew - also named Sathyaraju - who had come to stay at the ashram in 1978 and was very affectionate and attached to Seenu and had been very helpful around the ashram, came and opened the door and then gave him some food which he had kept as *prasadam*. He was in tears and was very upset as to why Seenu had gone away.

" *I couldn't explain to anybody why and how I was hurt. Some felt very sad, while some tried to criticize me, but two months later when Swamiji came there, after hearing all the story, immediately He understood me and ridiculed those responsible for troubling me. But then He took me inside His room and suddenly started scolding me! I was bewildered for a while and could not understand why Swamiji was so affectionate and understanding outside, and then after coming inside His room had started scolding me so suddenly. He gave me a dressing-down for about an hour while I quietly stood in front of Him, with Him scolding me with comments such as,*

'I will peel off your skin! I will throw you out!'

But throughout the ordeal, though I felt nervous and kept quiet, I never felt panicked or insecure because I knew Swamiji would never harm me. I thought that like an affectionate father He was trying to teach me some lesson.

After about an hour His anger suddenly vanished as quickly as it had come. He started smiling and then said affectionately, 'Idiot. Come and have some sweets. I know your mind,' adding,

'Do you know why I was scolding you? I know that you did not do anything wrong. Your only fault was - why did you give up your place and go away from the ashram? Why did you try to go away from Me? If people behave badly you can go inside your room and relax for a while, but this is not the way to deal with these things - by going away from the ashram. Never allow any egotistic things to enter your mind.'

That was a great lesson he taught me."

That year another mentally retarded boy was brought by his family members from Andra Pradesh to stay in the ashram. Swamiji wanted Seenu to look after him in addition to his first charge but it was much more difficult to take care of this new boy. He used to run away on the streets so that Seenu and Sathyaraju would have to run after him and bring him back. He would also keep soiling all over his body and his room so that three or four times a day Seenu had to wash and clean both the boy and his room. When Swamiji was there, a devotee who cared a great deal for Seenu approached Swamiji and told him that this newly-arrived boy was very dirty and was soiling everywhere and that he felt Seenu should not be made to clean all these things like this.

Swamiji replied, "Seenu is devoted to me. Do not stop him from doing these things. He is doing all these things willingly. This will remove all his *prarabdha karma* (acquired impressions of the mind)."

Considering it a service to his Divine Guru Swamiji, Seenu always felt very happy in attending to these mentally retarded boys. Seenu tried to look after this boy as best he could, but the boy also used to get epileptic fits and later developed complications in his liver which they tried to attend to medically. But eventually he became more ill despite medical treatment and finally passed away with Seenu holding him on his lap.

" *I tried to help his soul by singing God's glory and praying to my Divine Guru Swamiji to bless his soul. Though a mentally retarded boy, at least the soul was so fortunate to have got a chance to live in the ashram and breathe his last there.*"

The young boy passed away on 5th August 1979 and two days later the ashram was due to celebrate Swamiji's *tapas purti* (anniversary of His tapas). The ashram inmates informed Swamiji and the boy's relatives of his passing. Swamiji had asked that Seenu keep the body until either the relatives came or they permitted the ashram to perform the funeral. With the *tapas purti* celebrations due in two days, some members of the ashram management committee were concerned by the situation and created objections, saying that as long as the dead body was in the ashram it was not possible to hold any function - it is a tradition in India that such a thing would be considered unclean. So, unsure of what was best, that night Seenu telephoned Swamiji who was in Bangalore.

Swamiji was furious.

"Tell the committee that even if you die also, the body should be kept in a room and first attend to the function because it is for the public. Public service is more important; this is our Mission. The dead body can be attended to later. There is no such 'untouchability' for us. So even if the body needs to be kept, you should organize all the *bhajans*, mass feeding and functions properly."

Anybody was likely to misunderstand Swamiji's comments. By nature, Swamiji was totally outspoken and always gave a straight-forward, blunt answer.

But it was another great lesson for Seenu - that always the Mission devotees must keep service to the public in the forefront and that their own comfort or emotions should come second.

" Swamiji always said, 'Selfish people - those who bother about their own troubles and suffering - can never serve the public in the Mission. While serving the Mission we cannot afford to feel sorry for ourselves.' Such was the great strength of Swamiji's iron-will teachings."

Well, by the grace of the Divine Guru, the family did permit the funeral to be performed on the day before the *tapas purti* and the function then went on without any hindrance, but this gave Seenu a chance to learn another great lesson from his Guru.

Towards the end of that year Seenu got the chance to visit Swamiji's birthplace, Adivarapupeta, for the first time. The Maharani of Patna's grandchildren were studying in a public school in Dehra Dun and Swamiji asked Seenu to accompany them on their journey home for the holidays; so Seenu and Sathyaraju went with them. While in Bhubaneswar, Swamiji ordered Seenu to visit the nearby pilgrimage town of Puri which has the famous Shrine of Lord Vishnu's incarnation, Sri Jaganath.

While he was a teenager, Seenu had found great solace in going to temples and had enjoyed the quietness and the calm vibrations of the sacred grounds. However once he found his Guru in 1971, Seenu's mind had become totally engulfed by His presence all the time and He was Seenu's God, Guru, Father, Mother, and everything, so he found that he never felt like going to temples after that or even worshipping any other form of God. Though he used to sing *bhajans* in the name of all forms of God, in every form Seenu found that he saw his beloved Swamiji. Whenever devotees used to come to Dehra Dun during Swamiji's stays there, they would often go to visit famous near-by pilgrimage Shrines like Bhadrinath, Kedaranath, and so on.

Every time Swamiji used to tell Seenu, "If you wish you can also go for a pilgrimage with them."

He always declined, explaining, "Swamiji, my pilgrimage is Your Lotus Feet. It is a rare chance that you are here physically. I don't want to miss that rarest opportunity and go anywhere else."

He found he felt like going along only if Swamiji Himself went. Near-by Rishikesh and Haridwar were places where Swamiji would take the devotees for a bath in the Ganges and to Seenu it always seemed like the *gopis* (cow-maids) playing with Lord Krishna. Swamiji used to play like a child, throwing water on everyone and forcing everyone to take a dip in the water. In that way He bestowed spiritual blessings on the devotees.

Hence when Swamiji directed Seenu to have the *darshan* of Lord Jaganath in Puri, Seenu went with some slight reticence. Obeying Swamiji's direction however, he visited the temple and paid his respects to the deities there. He respectfully approached the *vigrahams*(idols) and took *namaskaram* (prostration), but to his astonishment when he looked back up at the idol, he found it was no longer there, but had been replaced by the smiling, glowing figure of his Divine Guru, Shivabalyogi! At whichever deity's shrine

Seenu visited within the temple he found Swamiji's form appeared to him at the place of the presiding deity's idol. Again taking *namaskaram* he came away astounded and elevated by the experience. His dear Swamiji was indeed Lord Jaganath!

From here Seenu travelled with Swamiji to Adivarapupeta and during his stay there, another of the dreams which he used to have very often both before and after coming to the ashram, became a real experience in this world. At Adivarapupeta, inside the *dhyana mandir* (meditation room) where Swamiji performed His 12 years of *tapas*, the great *Yogi* had later installed the idols of goddess Parvati and a Shivalingam with the name of Lord Vaidyanatheshwar. While they were at the ashram, Swamiji instructed Seenu to have a bath early each morning and be ready at the temple at 3.30, and Swamiji Himself used to also come there at that time. Seenu had the great good fortune to be able to pour water and then milk from a large vessel as *abhishekam* (bathing) to the Lingam while Swamiji very affectionately, like a child to his father, would give a bath to Lord Shiva.

" *That was like being in Lord Shiva's abode of Kailas. Swamiji always used to ask me to sing* Lingashtakam *(song in praise of Shivalingam) which He was very fond of. Singing the* Lingashtakam ' Brahma Murari ... ' *it was a supreme bliss because so many times Swamiji had come into my dreams and made me perform* abhishekam *to the Shivalingam. Silently I would watch Swamiji's face as He used to do* abhishekam *to the Shivalingam in the temple at Adivarapupeta and give a bath to Lord Shiva. This was the most sublime sight I ever witnessed in my whole life. It was a great bonus blessing to do the* abhishekam *while Swamiji Himself gave a bath to the Shivalingam.*"

The pouring was a difficult task as the vessel was sometimes extremely heavy and Seenu found that as he poured water on the Shivalingam, the vessel's weight would surprisingly increase - so much so that Seenu thought he would drop it. Swamiji sometimes used to yell things like, "Don't drop the vessel", "Hold it higher", "Keep it straight" but also would lovingly encourage his disciple, "I know your hands must be hurting. Don't worry, just keep looking over here. "

" *On one morning I was holding the large pot and pouring the water over the Shivalingam, and the vessel appeared to become increasing heavy to the point where I thought I would not be able to hold it any longer. I continued on but had nearly reached my physical limits and try as I may, did not feel I could hold it any longer. Just at the point of collapse, Swamiji started to sweetly sing the* Lingashtakam *as the* abhishekam *continued and wonderously the vessel began to lighten so that I could hold it safely.*"

During the sojourn here in Adivarapupeta, Swamiji once went to near-by Kakinada to see and bless the ailing mother of a close devotee and on the return journey the car broke down. So leaving it behind where it had stopped in the forest Swamiji was brought to the ashram by another car. Next day Swamiji sent Seenu and some devotees back to the car saying that the car's springs had to be taken for repair.

"Because the car is in the midst of the forest, go and look after the car until the work is done."

Before they left, jokingly Swamiji asked Seenu, "The car is in the midst of the forest so you may not get food for a long time. Is it alright with you, or will you cry?"

Seenu replied, "No problem, Swamiji. If we chant your name in the midst of a forest also, from somewhere the food will come."

So the small band went and stayed there with the car for the whole day. The two devotees who were with Seenu eventually could not wait any longer for nourishment and set off, saying that they would try to find some food; but Seenu decided to stay with the car as he had promised his Guru. He waited and waited. A long time passed since the others had departed and still there was no sign of their return.

Suddenly from inside the forest a person appeared and after looking at Seenu, asked if he was hungry and gave him some *dhosas* (lentil pancakes) to eat. Seenu could only see it as the Grace of his Divine Guru, and ate them and felt his hunger quite satisfied. Sometime later the two other devotees who had ventured off, arrived back with some *oopma* (semolina savoury) which they gave him and he also ate some of that.

After a further hour two devotees arrived from the ashram with dinner - some tasty *palaharam* (sweets) and *rasam (pepper soup)*. They said that Swamiji was worried they might not have eaten any food at all for the whole day.

" *Such was His Grace and kindness.*"

11

Seenu Runs Away

For many years it was difficult for Seenu to manage the monetary needs of the ashram. Four or five people were staying in the ashram and it was totally dependent on devotees' donations - there were often not sufficient funds. For a long time it was very difficult to look after the maintenance, pay the bills for electricity, phone and so on. Sometimes when there was no gas for simple cooking, Seenu and Sathyaraju, taking the mentally retarded boy, would go into the forest area to fetch firewood for cooking. Vegetables, oil - all these things were a luxury for them. They had to use everything very carefully but because of Swamiji's Grace, mentally they never felt any hardship and enjoyed every situation even when things were tough. This taught them to adjust and manage by keeping their requirements to a minimum. Every year when Swamiji came to the ashram some donations would be made and Swamiji used to also help financially, but then the ashram had to manage with those donations for the remainder of the year.

" *I knew Swamiji wanted to train me in every way. Just as I had learnt harmonium and drum, worship and meditation, Swamiji wanted me to also learn accounts work and look after the office. Accounts and mathematics were always a headache for me but when it came to the service of the Mission, with determination I learnt and tried to manage with whatever meager resources were available. I enjoyed the service of white-washing the ashram walls, cleaning the toilets and cleaning the ashram and its surrounds as*

Swamiji always emphasized on sacrificing the ego of belonging to any higher caste, creed or status. Personally also I never felt any difference in caste, creed or status. I always believed in the higher principles as taught by the great saint Purandara Dasa who had sung,

'You cannot get any liberation unless and until you become a slave to your Guru and obey His commands and take everything that He gives in life - good and bad, gain or punishment - as His Grace and blessings.' "

Once in 1980 it became very difficult to manage the ashram finances and it occurred to Seenu that perhaps he should buy a lottery ticket. He reasoned if a couple of 100,000 Rp came by a lottery windfall, it could be put into a fixed deposit in the bank and the ashram finances could be managed on the interest earned. He simply thought how nice it would be if they won the lottery so that he could manage the ashram peacefully. So for two to three months regularly Seenu bought lottery tickets but, perhaps luckily, no lottery prize came.

Now Swamiji came to Dehra Dun in the summer months on His annual trip and on the day after He arrived Seenu was giving Him an oil massage. Though fearful that He might scold him, Seenu just wanted to convey to Him that as it had become so difficult to manage the ashram funding that he had thought of buying some lottery tickets, but had not won any money.

" *When I told Him what I had done Swamiji who was lying down on the ground, suddenly got up and hit me on the head with His left hand. I felt very giddy in the head for a while and saw stars, as His left hand was very strong. The next 1½ to 2 hours was His yelling and scolding.*

'You forget that you are a sannyasi. *You should never go after money. Should never allow the mind to worry about money. One day money will come on its own, when you don't have any desires. Never try to go after money yourself.'*

Finally Swamiji said as a blessing, 'Do not worry. The ashram will run - as much as is required will always come.'

That proved to be His Grace and blessings as after that, though we did not have much money in the ashram, all work went smoothly and from somewhere the contributions used to come - as much as was required to hold functions and organize mass feedings and to run the ashram's daily needs."

At one time when Seenu was in the Bangalore ashram during a sojourn in the south, whenever Swamiji would have His oil massage in a small room adjacent to His living room Seenu would usually go to His room to dust and clean. While in the room doing the cleaning he would often take sweets or an apple from the fridge and go about dusting the room, while preparing the hot water for Swamiji's bath. One day he started the oil massage and some other devotees joined in and so Seenu was able to leave and go to Swamiji's room and start the dusting and cleaning.

When he looked in the fridge he saw a milk cake there, so he took a piece as usual and continued dusting. Suddenly Swamiji thought to check what he was doing in the room, so He came in and there saw Seenu - with a broom in one hand, cake in the other, and merrily singing Swamiji's name!

Swamiji declared, "Naughty boy! Look at him - I knew he would be eating. He started the massage and then came here and started eating!"

As punishment, He made Seenu eat a huge piece of milk cake - so much that it made him feel quite sick.

Although he liked sweets, Seenu's greater motivation for these larcenous episodes was more subtle than appeared to the casual observer. It was not the sweets themselves that were so important to him but that the closeness of his relationship with his Guru made him feel he belonged to Him and therefore there was no sense of separateness. Thus the taking of the sweets exemplified this sense of belonging he had in his relationship with Swamiji, like a son with his father. He would quietly go on eating because of the secure feeling of belonging to Him.

And for all this eating Swamiji never seriously scolded Seenu though He did tease and make fun of him. The Guru would sometimes tell observers jokingly, "This is the tax he charges Me for his services."

On another occasion somebody had brought a large serving of salted, roasted cashew nuts, and jokingly Swamiji told some nearby devotees, "Let me pour all these cashew nuts onto a plate, and build it up into a *gopuram* (temple spire shape) and then I will measure it's height every day. I will show you - this *gopuram* will lose height every day", and of course His prediction came true. Seenu would eat some every day and became fond of Swamiji's light-hearted teasing which also followed each day - it only increased his feeling of belonging to his beloved Guru.

Sometimes in the northern ashram Swamiji would also tease Seenu and make fun by telling devotees from south India who visited Dehra Dun and saw the fair-complexioned young disciple for the first time, "Seenu is an American boy who I have adopted."

But He worked untiringly in training and preparing His devotee for his *sadhana* and Mission. Sometimes when he was heavily scolding Seenu, He used to say,

"Many times I tell you and keep scolding. You don't listen to me. You'll have to be careful about the public. Don't become too friendly with anyone, because 10 - 15 years later when I will not be here physically, when you will have to look after and run the Mission, you will understand the difficulties I Myself had to face." Many of His words have proved prophetic.

Swamiji was in Dehra Dun at one time and one of Seenu's cousins was travelling to the pilgrimage town of Benares and so visited Dehra Dun on his way to take Swamiji's blessings. He was going to Benares because it was said in Seenu's family lineage, that his great grandfather Ishwara Poundareeka Dikshitar during his last days had left home by taking *sannyas* (monkhood) and went away, saying he would spend his last days in Benares. So

Seenu's cousin was travelling to Benares to try to locate the *samadhi* (tomb) there. After the cousin left the ashram on his forward journey, Swamiji suddenly turned to Seenu and pronounced, "Look in the same way, a time will come when your brother's grandchildren and their children will come to Dehra Dun in a pilgrimage to have *darshan* of your *samadhi*."

When Swamiji was staying in the Dehra Dun ashram during October 1981, He was invited by a devotee to visit Chamba in the state of Tehri Garhwal, so His disciple General Hanut Singh organized an army jeep to take Swamiji there. Any opportunity to travel with Swamiji was always an enjoyable spiritual experience and Seenu was to join the group on the journey. After first reaching Rishikesh they all bathed in the sacred river Ganges, with Swamiji as usual playing with them in the water like a child, though all were aware of the great spiritual blessings being poured on them at the time.

Leaving Rishikesh the party then proceeded on to Chamba with the General seated next to the driver and Swamiji sitting beside him also in the front seat as the jeep travelled along the narrow, winding, hilly roads. The rest of the group were sitting in the back seat, with Seenu sitting directly behind Swamiji.

" *Swamiji was seated in the front with His eyes closed, perhaps absorbed in the Self. Suddenly the door of the jeep on Swamiji's side sprang open and Swamiji's body, losing its support, lurched sideways. Instantly I shouted out, 'Swamiji !' and the driver brought the vehicle to a screeching halt. For a moment all of us were bewildered, thinking that Swamiji could have fallen off the edge of the mountain! However by the Divine Grace nothing happened to our beloved Swamiji as His hand was firmly holding the handle in front of the seat and General Hanut Singh managed to help Swamiji back into His seat.*

He simply looked at all of us and laughingly said, 'Hey were all of you frightened?' Further waving his hands He declared,

'Don't worry. I am not going to die in any accident like this. I will only go in samadhi.*'*

Relieved, we continued the journey finally reaching Chamba safely by Swamiji's Grace and later that night held a beautiful program to celebrate the great Yogi's arrival. "

Although his sense of belonging and his love for Swamiji was all-encompassing, Seenu did often experience great difficulties in relationships with others in the group of Swamiji's devotees. While so many were very affectionate and supportive, some through their own weakness found in him a focus for attack.

Once some devotees had whispered into Swamiji's ears some contrived stories in an effort to make it appear as if Seenu was solely responsible for a problem which had arisen in the Mission. When the *Yogi* came to Dehra Dun He was furious with Seenu and went on scolding him for two to three hours continuously and told Seenu that He had lost faith in him. Such a thing made the young disciple feel extremely miserable and dejected. For the first time Seenu thought that Swamiji had misunderstood him and that he should even leave the ashram and end his life somewhere in the forest. He felt absolutely deserted and alone. Perhaps to help him lose the ego and make him a better, more refined person, deliberately his Master used to scold him in front of others. Whereas some devotees tried to help Seenu by explaining the events to Swamiji, several other sycophants took this as an opportunity to blame him and try to see that he was sent away from the Dehra Dun ashram. Even after the admonishment was over, for several days afterwards Swamiji appeared totally annoyed with Seenu.

" *Though it was mentally very traumatic for me, in the end of this drama finally I realized it was a divine play by Swamiji to help me to renounce my attachment to Him physically and make me feel my beloved Swamiji within me and everywhere.*

On the first day He scolded me it was so tiring and traumatic mentally that when I retired to my room after the harrowing dressing down, my head felt so hot I poured 10 to 20 buckets of water over my head to cool it down. I took a couple of sleeping pills to have a sound sleep to recuperate. At that moment I really didn't have any idea of ending my life. When I did not get up until the evening, one devotee came to the room and tried to wake me up and I must have told him in my sleepy state, 'Let me sleep for some more time.'

Hearing this and seeing the pill bottle, the devotee misconstrued the situation and made a big scene and started shouting, 'Seenu is trying to commit suicide! He's taken sleeping pills!'

Word went to Swamiji and He became more furious. A doctor was called and he gave me salty water to make me vomit and it unnecessarily became a big drama. As nobody was ready to listen to me, I just kept quiet and did not bother to explain. At that time only General Hanut Singh, a very senior disciple of my Guru, understood me and took very good care of me and helped me to overcome the mental trauma. He was always trying to help me by talking to Swamiji, explaining, 'There has been some misunderstanding about Seenu. He needs to be given a chance to clarify what really happened.'

Just at that time I received news that my mother was not well and so taking this as an excuse, I thought I would go home and there I would go away somewhere in the forest and end my life. When I said I wanted to go, though Swamiji did permit it He was not really happy that I was leaving. Though I did not express to Him that I was intending to go away forever, as a Yogi Master he must have smelt my intention.

When I went to take leave of Swamiji, He tried to express His unhappiness that I was going.

'Your mother is seriously ill and maybe she is no more. Perhaps if that is so, then they won't keep the body until you reach home and so then what is the use of going there? There is so much work here to do and you have responsibilities here.'

But my mind was adamant that I should not stay there after so much misunderstanding. So I kept quiet, keeping my head bent when He was talking thus. When I finally took leave of Swamiji, I went to Bangalore to stay with my mother for some time. Within a week I started missing Swamiji and felt like crying and would actually bang my head on the wall from distress. Quietly I used to cry and pray to God to change my mind - that I wanted to go back to my Guru. I prayed to God,

'My mind has become stubborn not to go to the Guru but I really want to go back to Him because without my Guru, there's no meaning for my life and there is no meaning to be alive in this world.'

Almost every day Swamiji was coming into my dreams in different ways.

In one dream He told me, 'I have been scolding you and you have gone away from me. My scolding is not new to you, so why did you leave me and go away?'

In another dream I was running away and then I saw Swamiji running after me. He grabbed me by the hand and pulled me back. He tied me to a pole by a rope then graciously smiled at me, "saying affectionately ,'Now this is good'. I'm very happy that 'you cannot run away.' "

In a further dream I was trying to jump from a mountain top when suddenly Swamiji appeared and pulling me back, slapped me, saying, 'What nonsense are you doing? For a little bit of trouble in this world, if you abruptly end this life then you will have to face much more dangerous calamities after a death like this. You need to keep your mind very strong.'

Now with me staying in Bangalore and yearning for Swamiji, finally by Swamiji's Grace it was General Hanut Singh who became instrumental for me to return. From Bangalore I wrote to him my intention - that I wanted to simply go away into the forest, with Swamiji in my heart. Immediately he wrote back to me that he had spoken to Swamiji and that Swamiji really liked me and that I must come back because the General knew how much I loved my Guru. He wrote to me that I would regret it later if I went away.

Within my mind's turmoil, I however knew clearly that I could not live without Swamiji. This letter of the General's was the catalyst for my return. Immediately I started from Bangalore and came back to my Guru's abode in Dehra Dun ashram."

Later Mataji Kailash Kumari Devi, who always had been very affectionate to Seenu, explained to Swamiji that there has been some misunderstanding about all this and that he needed Swamiji's blessings. She also gave Seenu a lot of inspiration and encouragement, saying that he should not go away like that, but should stay with his Guru and fulfill his life's aim and the promise he had made to his mother.

Thus by the Divine Guru Swamiji's Grace, Seenu overcame this dreadful period and returned closer to his beloved Guru than ever.

12

Swamiji's Last Years

Swamiji came to Dehra Dun physically for the last time during the winter months of 1989 and stayed in Dehra Dun for two months, from mid-October to mid-December. During this visit He gave Seenu so much love and care and so many instances of spiritual advice and as always He was fond of feeding him. That year He insisted that all the devotees be given breakfast in front of Him. One day when one devotee chose not to eat a particular item, Swamiji pulled him up, "Why are you not eating this when I'm giving you this *prasad*? When tomorrow comes you may not get this chance at all!" These words of Swamiji's served as a prophecy and physically He never came back to Dehra Dun again after this visit.

Once many years before when they made an excursion to Rishikesh, Swamiji took a Shivalingam-shaped stone from the river Ganges and gave it to Seenu declaring, "This is your Guru's Guru. Keep it with you and worship it. All the Grace and blessings of the Divine will be bestowed upon you." Later when General Hanut Singh was constructing his cottage within the ashram campus, a mason who was working on the building became very attached to Seenu. Although he was Muslim and people following that faith do not perform ritual worship, when he saw Seenu performing his worship to this Shivalingam with such devotion and care, he carved another stone Shivalingam and presented it to him. Thus Seenu continued to worship both these Shivalingams and felt supremely peaceful. Every year when Swamiji came Seenu used to pray to

Him to perform worship to these Shivalingams, but Swamiji always used to tease and refuse, "I can do worship only when a temple has been built for these Shivalingams." When Swamiji came in 1989 one day when He came downstairs to go for a walk, Seenu, mustering all his courage again requested of Swamiji, "I don't have money to construct a temple for these Shivalingams. Please worship and bless them." Though he was expecting Swamiji to refuse once again, and probably yell and shout at him, to Seenu's surprise the *Yogi* took His hiking stick and struck both the Shivalingams three times each in a baptizing way, saying, "I have filled these Shivalingams with life and Shankar Bhagavan (Lord Shiva) will help you in your Mission and to develop this ashram also."

During the next year, 1990, in the beginning of August, Swamiji and His assistant were returning from an American tour when His flight had landed in Kuwait for re-fueling enroute to India just at the time that Iraq attacked Kuwait and He was held up in Kuwait for nearly 25 days.

By 1991 His health was proving to be in decline with His physical body showing signs of kidney failure and requiring dialysis regularly and Seenu started wondering if Swamiji was preparing to drop His physical body. He remembered Swamiji saying many times, "I have done *tapas* for all your sakes, and will establish ashrams well and then disappear from this world physically. All of you will have to run the Mission and take care of the ashrams." Because of Swamiji's body's deteriorating health, His tours were restricted to only places near to his south Indian bases but many hundreds and thousands came for His *darshan* in Bangalore. Swamiji always advised devotees that He would be with them in their hearts at all times.

When Seenu heard that Swamiji was ill he naturally wanted to visit Swamiji and regularly telephoned Swamiji to ask if he could visit Him in Bangalore. For reasons known only to Swamiji every time Seenu asked to visit Him Swamiji refused permission, directing him instead to stay back in the Dehra Dun ashram and look after it and instructing him, "You can always see Me within your heart."

Perhaps Swamiji thought that Seenu might not be able to take the sight of His physical illness and might be troubled by seeing it. Finally in 1993 after He undertook a 40 day *kayakalpa tapas* (body-regenerating sadhana) He finally permitted Seenu to visit Him in Bangalore. For a while Swamiji's body appeared to improve in health though He continued to be on dialysis. Every day Seenu saw Swamiji smiling and joking as He went about the daily routine and trying to keep everyone's morale high - mighty soul that He was and is.

" *I thought Swamiji did not want to disturb my devotion to Him, nevertheless I always felt Swamiji within me continuously guiding my meditations. In 1993 I saw Him always enthusiastic. He was always talking positively to me also. Swamiji was always absorbed in His real Self and never showed any of the fatigue of His physical illness. He was continuing all the programs as if nothing was happening to His physical body. Even on a day when His body would undergo dialysis for several hours He would still give darshan for many hours and continued meeting devotees, listening to everyone's problems with all the patience and continued to bless them with love and* vibhuti.

I felt closer than ever. As the days were nearing for me to leave Bangalore and return to Dehra Dun, a couple of days before I was to leave - it was a Sunday evening after programs and arathi *and the devotees served food. Swamiji always insisted that all the devotees be fed in front of Him. Throughout my life with Swamiji I saw He never took food first for Himself, but always insisted that all the devotees be fed first. After watching them eating peacefully He used to feel satisfied and go in and have His food. He used to say that His mother taught Him thus, because Swamiji was a very important personality, everyone would feed Him but would be likely to ignore and neglect other devotees so He always wanted to see that all the devotees were fed properly first. Every day in the ashram also He used to ask all of us whether we had food properly or not. Once Swamiji explained as to how He came to know in His childhood that the family was poor. He narrated how as a child, even at the age of four or five, He used to feel very hungry and every one or two hours He would ask His mother to give Him some food to eat and she kept something aside ready always for Him. When Swamiji was five years old it suddenly occurred to Him one day, 'I have not ever seen mother eating her food.'*

So one day Swamiji insisted that His mother also eat with Him. At first His mother refused, saying that she had work to do and she would eat later and that Swamiji should eat the food without her. But He insisted stubbornly that she must also eat with Him. Finally His mother agreed and served some food for herself on a plate and said, 'Look I have served this food for myself but have some jobs to finish. You have your food.' Thus saying she put the plate with the food inside the pantry. After eating His food, Swamiji as a child thought, 'I must see whether mother will really eat her food or not.'

So He hid Himself behind the door and waited there for nearly two hours but still His mother never ate the food which she had served for herself. After two hours, when she came back home, Swamiji quietly slipped out from behind the door where he was hiding and came in the front door as if he had also gone out somewhere and had just returned. When He asked as usual for some food from His mother she readily gave that food she had earlier kept aside for herself. Then Swamiji argued with her, 'Why didn't you eat this food you served for yourself?' He was surprised to see this made tears run down her cheeks and perturbed by this, Swamiji started wondering how he had offended His mother by asking her to eat. As He had lost His father when he was a small boy of 6 months old, whenever He had any confusion He always consulted His uncle. When he sought his counsel, His uncle explained to Him, 'Look boy, we are poor people. After your father's death, your mother has been working very hard so that she can feed you all.' But His uncle also advised the little boy that there was no need to feel shame because of this poverty, saying,

'Poverty is only a condition of circumstances and is no cause for shame. By hard work and honesty, one can overcome poverty.' That day, with total determination, Swamiji decided that from henceforth He would work to look after His mother so that she would not have to work anymore.

After annadannum *(mass feeding) Swamiji went inside and we all cleaned the hall, and as the cleaning was coming to an end I went to my room to change my clothes and to wash, but by then Swamiji had come back to the hall and saw that I was not there. He was furious as He thought that I had gone without helping the others to clean the hall. When I was coming back I saw Swamiji walking towards the temple and he appeared very annoyed with me and went on scolding me for nearly 45 minutes then and there. That day while He was scolding me, very strangely He said, 'When we all come to your ashram in Dehra Dun don't we all work? You should also be working here like that.' I never tried to argue with Swamiji and never tried to explain anything also. I did not want to infuriate Him more and also took all His scoldings as His love and blessings. He did not continue on to the temple but scolding me, he brought me back to the hall. All the other boys were having prasad. Suddenly Swamiji cooled down and said to me affectionately, 'Have this* prasad *poor boy', and He gave the* prasad *He had kept separately for me.*

Next day early morning when I was coming, I saw Swamiji in the garden with a devotee. Thinking that He might still be annoyed with me, instead of going near Him, I went to His room to clean it and the bathroom. When I entered the room I saw some sweets on the windowsill and took a piece to feel more secure about Swamiji. When I was cleaning the bathroom Swamiji sent the devotee to see what I was doing in the room, saying that I might be eating something. Always Swamiji used to tease me, saying, 'These sweets are the tax that I have to pay him.' When that man came I was cleaning the bathroom. He told me, 'Please go and be with Swamiji in the garden as He's done and I have to leave for work.' When we returned to Him that devotee told

Swamiji, 'Poor Seenu was cleaning the bathroom and was not eating anything.'

Swamiji turned to me with a quizzical look and asked, 'Is it true that you did not eat anything there?', so I replied that I took one piece of the sweets on the windowsill when I entered the room.

He laughed and said affectionately, 'I know my boy very well. Without taking some tax he won't be working.' Then after the devotee left Swamiji was talking to me for some time and showed me a small tree and said that it had been brought from Sri Lanka.

Then suddenly He directed me, 'Go and count all the mango trees and tell me how many there are.' So I went and counted them thoroughly and found there were about 170 small mango trees planted, so I came back and reported to Swamiji that there were 170 trees.

He exclaimed, 'Ay Badmash! (Hey Idiot!) One hundred and seventy! Come, let us count!'

I knew Swamiji had undergone dialysis the previous evening and so I told Him, 'Please keep sitting - I'll go and count again', but He persisted,

'No, no. You will go and tell me there are 270! Let us go together,' and insisted on coming with me.

Then Swamiji and I went on counting and to my amazement there were only 70!

I looked at Swamiji with a foolish smile, 'Swamiji, where have 100 trees gone?'

'Has someone eaten them? he queried, 'You said 170 !'

Astonished and confused, I could only say, 'It was definitely 170; I don't know what happened.'

In a teasing manner He replied, 'Then where are they - Who did this magic?' to which I answered, 'This must be Your Divine Play - How can I understand all this?'

Unconcerned He simply told me, 'OK, we have a job to do. Come with Me', and then led me behind His room and carrying a ladder in one hand, asked me to hold the other end. We put the ladder up into the mango tree that was behind His room. Another boy came there and Swamiji asked him to get a 'chopper' to trim the branches but after the boy left on his errand Swamiji told me, 'Quietly to go my room and you will see a chopper lying under my cot. Quickly bring it here before this boy returns,' so I went to His room and returned with the chopper Swamiji had described. With Swamiji holding onto the ladder He then asked me to climb up and chop off some extra branches. Now whenever He gave me work to do Swamiji was fond of teasing me during the task and this would always make me nervous. So Swamiji started shouting, 'Be careful! Don't chop the branch with the mangoes on it,' and of course, lo! - I chopped a branch laden with mangoes, which fell to the ground.

Now the ashram management had made a rule that if anyone picked flowers or fruit without permission they would be fined 100Rp.

Swamiji shouted, 'Come down quickly. Now we both will be fined 100Rp by the management!' and told me to quietly and quickly hide the mangoes under the cot in His room.

Afterwards we went inside. Some other devotees joined me and we gave an oil massage to Swamiji and also gave Him a bath. After the bath Swamiji's lady disciple Yashoda brought breakfast and Swamiji jokingly said, 'Look Amma*(mother), we both surrender. This mischief happened. I can pay 100 Rp no problem but Seenu doesn't have any money - from where can he pay, poor boy? So instead of a fine we can punish Seenu by getting him to eat 3 sour mangoes.'*

Sour mangoes are extremely difficult to eat and make one feel violently sick even after only a small serving, so to eat three whole fruits sounded like a torture. I thought, 'I'm going to die eating these three sour mangoes!'

Then Swamiji suggested, 'Look I will give you one idea. Take this coconut, which is sweet. Take one bite from the sour mango and then one bite from the sweet coconut and going on like this you can finish eating these three mangoes as punishment,' and roared with laughter.

Somehow by His blessings I was able to eat the torturous fruit and when I finished He said affectionately, 'Look in your life always in the beginning if you have something sour or bitter, you will definitely have a sweet life later!'

By these words I think Guru Maharaj showered His Grace and blessings. A couple of hours later I was to leave for Dehra Dun. At my departure He gave me some more coconuts to be passed as Prasad *to the devotees in Dehra Dun.*

I took a very emotional leave from Swamiji and was wondering whether I would ever be able to see Him again and indeed that proved to be my last meeting physically with my beloved Swamiji Guru Maharaj.

The care and love He showered on me, the practical teachings that He poured out to me and the inspiration He gave to be more determined was immense and I was always fortunate to receive them. "

13

Swamiji's Mahasamadhi

After that last meeting in Bangalore in 1993 Seenu returned to the ashram in Dehra Dun and carried on his duties. In the beginning of 1994, he heard that Swamiji was going to Adivarapupeta for Mahashivaratri and that He was likely to come North and spend sometime in Dehra Dun after that. Aware of the precarious health of His physical body, Seenu constantly prayed to God to grant health to his Guru's physical body so that He could continue to be with the devotees for a long time to come.

" *I was quite excited in hearing that He might come to Dehra Dun after Mahashivaratri in 1994. However in March 1994 we heard He had postponed the trip due to health conditions. That was really not good news.* "

During the last week of March Seenu travelled to Delhi at the invitation of the devotees there to participate in the monthly kirtan program. Returning by bus on March 28th Seenu's mind was, as ever, constantly thinking of his Guru but the thoughts this time were of a different nature; a feeling was developing that some important event was about to occur.

" *About five minutes after I reached Dehra Dun ashram in the evening, the news which we never wanted to hear finally came. A devotee telephoned the ashram to convey to us that our beloved Swamiji Guru Maharaj had dropped His physical body to go into*

Mahasamadhi[33]. *That same night I rushed back to Delhi with some devotees and left directly for Adivarapupeta by train. When we reached Adivarapupeta ashram after the three day journey, we found Swamiji's physical body had been placed in the compound of the ashram on an elevated dais, on a chair. For long time I was gazing at the body. Every moment that I had spent physically at the Lotus Feet of my beloved Guru came flooding back to my memory. Every teaching that He gave, the love and care, and that so many times I had the chance to give Him oil massages, baths and food. Everything was now history.*

Since the first day that I saw Him in 1971 when I was instantly drawn to Him there was really never confusion that He was and is, one with God, as All-Pervading, Omnipresent, Divine Spirit. "

However there was confusion amongst some devotees at the ashram. Various people were claiming to be in trance and some were saying that Swamiji would come back to the physical body. All the devotees gathered and tried to discuss the matter of whether to keep the *Yogi's* body unburied. At that point Seenu remembered an incident that happened during Swamiji's stay in Dehra Dun in 1977 when a local saint was said to be in *samadhi* and some devotees felt he would return to the physical body later, but Swamiji had firmly refuted this idea saying that if the body had given way there is no question of the soul coming back to that body. Swamiji had instructed people then that the body needs to be physically examined and one should see if there was any glow on the face. The story had unfolded like this.

There was a saint who lived nearby in Dehra Dun and suddenly his secretary announced to his devotees that the Guru was in *samadhi*, had gone to another world and would be returning only quite some time later. Several months passed by and during

---

[33] *Mahasamadhi* - 'Great Samadhi' - The final event in which a *Yogi* drops the physical body and merges totally with the Divine.

this time only the secretary was allowed into the saint's room - all other devotees were not permitted to even see the saint. Then some of these devotees grew suspicious and were trying to obtain the help of other saints in the area to check that everything was proper. Then a group of them came to Swamiji and requested His help in trying to find out what was happening - whether the saint was really in *samadhi*. The saint's secretary had threatened them by saying that the saint would curse anyone who disturbed him. But Swamiji assured them that no saint would curse anyone like that and advised them that they should force the secretary to allow them to see the body. Swamiji directed them to check for the life-glow on the face which is present during life and if necessary to take medical advice.

Following these instructions the group attempted to check the body but again the secretary blocked their attempts and so they returned and requested Swamiji to come there. Then at the invitation of those devotees Swamiji went and ordered that the secretary open the room telling him that he need not worry that He would be cursed.

After some initial resistance the secretary finally opened the doors and Swamiji saw the body had become black and there was no glow or aura of any life at all. After five minutes meditation there Swamiji blessed the saint, came out and told the devotees that their guru had dropped his physical body. He further instructed that if needed they should take medical advice and then take leave of the guru's physical body with due respect.

Finally in Adivarapupeta the committee and other senior devotees met and decided to perform the *Mahasamadhi* ceremony and take leave of Sri Shivabalayogi's physical body. His body was placed in the *Samadhi* (*Yogi's* tomb) with all the honours due to a Great One.

" *Standing there, I was trying to visualize what Ramakrishna Paramahamsa's disciples would have felt when he also attained*

Mahasamadhi.

After the Mahasamadhi *ceremony was over in Adivarapupeta there was definitely a feeling of loss and I thought that though He is omnipresent, yet we would miss His physical presence. We never thought it would be over so soon."*

Seeing all this disturbance surrounding the passing of Swamiji's physical form and more so the attendant commotion of people professing to be in trance and giving conflicting directions on how to deal with the passing and the handling of Swamiji's body, Seenu felt very disturbed. He was hurt and very sad at these goings-on and left Adivarapupeta shortly after the *Mahasamadhi* ceremony was completed and travelled to Bangalore. But instead of visiting his mother's home or Swamiji's ashram there, he journeyed straight on to Mysore and from there walked out to the Chamundi Hills where he had first had Swamiji's *darshan* and where he used to retire for solitude when a teenager. Swamiji had sometimes taken his devotees to a secluded area in the hills which He said was the place where Maharishi Markandeya had performed *tapas*. So Seenu returned to this quiet, secluded area away from all the distractions of the Mission, quietly sat and commenced *dhyana.*

" *Quietly I sat there for two or three days - I am not sure how long. Perhaps I was in deep meditation. Eventually I heard some sounds from nearby and coming out of this state suddenly to my amazement I saw Swamiji standing in front of me, his figure appearing surrounded by a dazzlingly bright ethereal light. I was struck dumb with wonder.*

He spoke to me, saying, 'Your time has come to do tapas. *The 20 years that you served selflessly has given you the fruits of seven years of* tapas *and if you do another five years* tapas *it will be enough.'*

At that time, I never had any thoughts of doing tapas *and was not even sure whether I would be able to sit at one place for such a long time. Regaining the ability to speak I answered that at this time I simply wanted to serve in Swamiji's mission, that I did not wish to perform* tapas *- I wanted simply to sing of Swamiji's glory and spread the knowledge of what a great* Yogi *Sri Shivabalayogi was and is.*

Swamiji smiled and continued, 'When the time is ripe, you will have to sit and circumstances will also force you, because of your prarabdha *(acquired impressions of the mind).'"*

With a final blessing directing him to return to Dehra Dun, the vision disappeared. Seenu simply sat thinking about it, astounded. He was not prepared to give too much credence to the vision; he was concerned that the vision might simply be an illusion created by his grieving mind - just a manifestation of a strong desire to see Swamiji again. However he also felt that if the experience had indeed been a genuine divine vision rather than an illusion then Swamiji would organize the circumstances such that the *tapas* would occur, just as He had said in the vision - so there was no need for him to be concerned about it for the time being.

Returning to Bangalore he went to be with his mother for two days and then stayed for a few days at the Bangalore ashram. Here, as at the Adivarapupeta ashram, confusion seemed to prevail amongst the devotees. Several devotees were trying to go into trance, declaring themselves to be Swamiji and attempting to instruct in their own way. Dejected with sadness at this behaviour Seenu thought it best to stay away from these things and returned - as the vision had also directed him - to the Dehra Dun ashram and continued his duties there.

For several months he continued his usual daily duties but an underlying current of sadness and grief haunted the days. He told no one else about the vision he had experienced in Mysore but simply continued to carry out his normal ashram responsibilities. He missed Sri Shivabalayogi tremendously and was constantly thinking of Him and remembering all the times he had shared with

Him and His kindness and guidance which had always been there.

All the time for the last 20 years his only reason for staying in this world had been his dear Swamiji and he now felt there was nothing left in this world to hold him here.

Finally after several months, on 5th November a function was being held at the Dehra Dun ashram to commemorate the late Maharani of Patna, Kailash Kumari Devi, who had been a great devotee of Swamiji's during her life and initially donated the ashram premises to Him.

"*I was performing* homan *when from the midst of the* homa kundam *(homam pit), Swamiji's brightly glowing form manifested again just as before in the Chamundi Hills.*

Smiling sweetly at me, He declared, 'The fifth day from now will be Kartik Shuklapaksham *(the eighth day after the full moon in the Indian month of* Kartik*). On that day I shall appear again and cause you to sit for* tapas.'

Once again I was wondering whether these were the visions of my own mental projections or what it could be. "

Just as Seenu had not told anyone about the first vision he had experienced, neither did he tell anyone of this vision either. He was unsure that he would be able to do *tapas*; he felt it might be simply beyond his physical and mental capacity to sit continuously in one place for several years. He was aware that it required extraordinary strength - both physical and mental strength - to be able to complete the grueling *sadhana* and he was also aware that several people had attempted *tapas* under Swamiji's guidance and some had found it so difficult that they had left the spiritual path completely. Some had even turned their back on their Guru. Yet his overpowering desire for Self-realization was also present and a desire to do *tapas* had slowly grown in his mind over the years, maturing almost unknown to him. So again he simply waited without telling anyone of his experience, certain that if it was real - if it wasn't just an illusion created by his mind's grief - then his Guru would guide him just as He had always done.

So it was that 5 days later, on 10th November 1994, after the evening *arathi* at the ashram just as Seenu finished the *puja* all of a sudden he saw the shining figure of Sri Shivabalayogi manifesting again, this time from the photo of Swamiji which was kept on the dais in the *darshan* hall.

" *The only physical anchor for my mind to be alive in this world had disappeared with the* mahasamadhi *of my beloved Swamiji. Everything appeared meaningless and I felt totally withdrawn. The dearest singing of* bhajans *in glory of my Guru and God also appeared lifeless. For a while the Mission appeared meaningless. The mind was wondering about the two strange manifested visions that I had experienced after Swamiji's* Mahasamadhi. *Not that Swamiji Himself had disappeared. Swamiji had become the Divine - omnipresent. Though the mind had accepted the reality, in a corner of the heart, the emotional vibrations of the mind did miss Swamiji and felt very miserable and it was at a loss for a while.*

Finally came that day, 10th November 1994 - Kartik Shuklapaksham. *In the evening as usual I did one hour of* bhajans *as a duty and performed the* arathi. *After the* arathi *as the mind kept wondering, suddenly from the dais the mind saw Swamiji coming down and touching me in between the eyebrows. It appeared as if He took me inside the room, made me sit down and asked me to keep my eyes closed. As I was closing my eyes, it felt as if I was sinking into a deep sea of space. Total darkness had engulfed, total silence and serenity was there. Nothing else seemed to be there. No thoughts were coming. In that state I heard a strong voice telling me,*

'Look, from this room either you have to come out as a Yogi, *or your dead body shall come out. Do not abandon the practice under any circumstances until you reach the goal. I want you to do this for five years as you already have the fruits of*

seven years tapas.*' A mantra also came, and then the voice asked me to face North.*

Thus it all started. "

14

Tapas

The *tapas* had commenced with Swamiji placing Seenu into a state of deep meditation in which the mind became stilled. The guidance He gave was two main directives:

" Slowly, skillfully, bring both the eyeballs to the point in between the eyebrows. You will have amazing results, "

and He added,

" When a vision or thought - anything - occurs in any form, in any potency, whether it's a mental projection, imagination, or a total physical manifestation, just do not try to analyze what it is. Do not try to make any judgments. Don't even recognize it. Simply watch. Focus your attention, let your mind be concentrated without any thoughts."

" *He further said,'* Just keep watching, whatever happens.' *So the mind had become alert to this command. The mind used to try to think something and then it would become alert on it's own, 'I should not think. I should not try to analyze what this is - whether it is dreadful, whether it is pleasant, whether it is blissful, or any visions that come.'*

The mind had learned not to analyze and gradually the eyeballs had come to a standstill, to the 'vanishing point', as I would like to call it in between the eyebrows, the brumadhya, *the* bhrikuti. "

The other people in the ashram of course had not been aware of Seenu's previous visions of Swamiji nor witnessed the manifestation of Swamiji this time and the initiation into *tapas*. It must have appeared quite odd when at the end of the evening *arathi* Seenu suddenly walked back into the room on the terrace adjacent to the hall, sat and closed his eyes. He did not stir that whole night or the next day or the next, and they must have thought that it might be that his mind, through the grief at his dear Guru's passing, had become disturbed. He did not open his eyes for two or three days but each day they brought something for him to eat and then later took it away, untouched. On the third day he returned to a waking consciousness and asked for some milk to drink, but then reverted to his *sadhana*.

As the days passed by General Hanut Singh, who as one of Swamiji's senior disciples had been permitted to build a cottage on the ashram campus, returned from his winter tour away. He had often been a champion for Seenu in the years of ashram life and when he heard about what had happened, he came and met the *tapaswin*.

When Seenu expressed to him that he didn't know whether he'd be able to continue or not, and that the ashram needed to be looked after (this was Swamiji's initial directive to him when he joined Swamiji's service), the General firmly encouraged him to continue, saying,

" These are not important and you must continue with *tapas*. Do not worry about the ashram. It will be looked after."

The meditation went on by itself and followed a daily pattern of periods of about seven to eight hour cycles.

From the early hours of the morning he would be in meditation through till about midday. After a short break it would re-commence and continue through until the late evening and then a third period would extend till the early morning again. At this early morning break he would have 15 to 20 minutes of exercise then take a bath and consume some light nourishment of milk before the cycles re-commenced. The periods of meditation were not timed but simply occurred as such, spontaneously.

" *Automatically I used to come out of meditation after a certain period. When I came out then I would realize there was enormous pain in the body, legs and back but the mind would not react to the pain. General Hanut Singh had instructed the ashram people to look after the body properly by massaging the hands and feet. Occasionally he used to come and meet me to enquire about my welfare and any needs, and encouraged me to proceed. As time passed by, many experiences came in the form of visions and manifestations. When they came, they appeared totally physical and solid. Gradually the mind was learning as it remained determined that, let death happen to the physical body, it shall not stop this* tapas *as there was nothing else left for me in this world.* "

To try understand a little of what *tapas* is, we can refer to his words when he later tried to give some clues as to what it involves.

" *If you try to hold the mind still, focused on one point for only a minute or two - for only a moment or two - you will find how difficult it is. However if one can focus the mind like this, single-pointedly focused on one point without any thoughts for one whole hour, then one is said to be meditating. If one can meditate like this for seven to eight hours at a stretch, then one is said to be performing* tapas. "

This gives some idea of the immense mental focus required. It is meditation in its highest pitch.

Meditation itself was of course not new to him. Within three or four years of coming to the ashram Seenu had already started sitting for at least four hours of meditation each day - two hours in the early morning hours and two hours in the late night. Furthermore when Swamiji used to come to Dehra Dun He would sometimes make Seenu sit for longer periods of meditation if the program for the day allowed it. So over the years the duration of his daily meditation increased beyond this four hours a day.

Also even when working in the Mission activities the disciple's mind was usually quiet and remained receded, never going into much agitation and was thus, by habit, in a meditative state. Even at times during his 20 years of service when he experienced frustration - when there was injustice or peoples' politics disturbed the functioning of the Mission - there might have been disillusionment sometimes. Yet the love and attachment to Swamiji, the Guru, was very, very strong and so the mind, even if disturbed briefly by such things, used to quickly come back to Swamiji's Lotus Feet and remain peaceful. Nothing really 'sat into' the mind for a very long time.

Therefore in those preceding twenty years he had been practicing meditation daily for an average of about five hours so that when the time was ripe and the Guru's Grace descended, it was thus possible for him to sit for at least seven hours at a time.

" Swamiji's manifestation used to appear once a month on every full moon day. Before the manifestation I would not know anything nor would I anticipate anything, as the mind did not remember anything. But every time the manifestation took place, I heard Swamiji telling me, 'I am your Divine Guru. I have come as today is full moon day.'

All the time whenever He appeared the mind remained dumbfound - I would not talk or ask anything but would simply would reply, 'Yes' or 'No' if Swamiji asked questions about any visions, temptations or fear.

Then He used to also reassure me, 'It will all disappear. Do not worry, as it all exists only in the mind. Nothing will happen to you.'

The mind had learned just simply to listen to whatever the Guru commanded without trying to analyze. It simply obeyed - it had learned to obey. So thus the mind had started becoming quiet, remaining in stillness, though a lot of visions and manifestations were occurring. "

For most of the time when performing *tapas* facing the North, he had very little trouble and few obstacles except that visions and some 'sound effects' were occurring sometimes. The sounds would be either like a thunderstorm or a bombing sound or a 'thud'. As they occurred abruptly they would jerk the mental concentration but he found that the mind would then quickly recover its concentration as it was becoming alert that these were simply illusions being created.

Swamiji had advised, "Illusions will be created to test your determination and to disturb your mind. Do not allow the mind's concentration to judge or analyze anything. Simply consider them as illusions and continue to focus the attention in between the eyebrows."

So the mind was alert to such disturbances and it used to reassure itself that they were simple illusory effects and that it shouldn't worry about them. The understanding also began to develop that even if anything happened to the body it was not a problem and there was no fear whatsoever in the entire period of *tapas*.

At this stage he was gradually losing awareness of the external sounds from the environment as the mind was becoming more concentrated, though he did experience pain in the body, legs and particularly headaches. But as the mind became more introverted the disturbance caused by these also reduced.

" *So gradually I could see the mind was coming totally into concentration. Gradually this was happening, that the mind though it was having a lot of visions and there used to be physical pains also sometimes (because during the first one or two years it was not that I totally lost outside awareness yet). Gradually the percentage of the mind going introverted was increasing, yet I still used to feel the physical pain sometimes. Some sounds used to disturb me sometimes but at all these times a strong determination and a deep* vairagya *(detachment) helped me not to discontinue the sittings. I never thought of getting up.*

When the pain used to occur so this determination also came to my mind, which Swamiji had taught,

'Either you should come out as a Yogi *or your dead body should come out. Put in efforts until the last breath of life.'*

So there was no question of abandoning the practice.

After the physical disappearance of Swamiji I felt, 'What is there for me in this world?' - because that attachment to Swamiji was the most precious thing for me. His physical presence was the greatest thing for me in this world. In fact that attachment was what really made me continue to live on this earth - otherwise, even from my childhood, I never liked to live in this world.

'Either', I used to think as a child, 'this world must be switched off or my life should come to an end. Then the problems will be over.' So it was only when I saw Swamiji that some attachment came and I fell in love with Him. For twenty years I had that rarest chance to serve Him very closely. He loved me like a mother and father and Guru.

Finally when the physical disappearance occurred, so this vairagya *occurred - 'What is there for me now? If one can become a* Yogi *that will be the greatest final achievement for which I had a yearning from my childhood.'*

So I never got disturbed. I continued. "

Apart from the 'sound effect' disturbances, many visions used to occur in this initial stage. While many *sadhaks* (those practicing *sadhana*) give great importance to the visions they experience, through Swamiji's training and from his readings of *Yoga Vasistha* he was aware of them - as with the 'sound effects' - as simply illusions created by the mind, generated from its own *samskaras* (previous impressions of the mind). Though many such visions came, following his Guru's advice he simply observed them and did not allow the mind to get caught up in them.

" *Just as one will get up after a dream sequence, the consciousness started realizing practically that the visions and manifestations were all its own conditions. When visions or manifestations appeared, it was as physical as you would see this world. Just like when you are dreaming, the dream appears so real and physically true. Only when you get up from the sleep then one realizes that it was a dream. Thus gradually the mind started losing interest in any such visions - whether good or bad. Gradually they all decreased and only Swamiji's manifestation continued to appear.*

About the visions and manifestations I can say this, based on my own experience.

I would describe the visions as occurring in three stages, depending on the level of concentration of the mind.

The first stage is the imagination of the mind. This imagination of the mind is not an ordinary thing. It is a capability if used in a controlled way. It is only with this imagination technology that the whole creation has taken place and the whole universe is run, and humanity has achieved so much in this world using this imagination power.

But if the imaginations are not under control and single pointed it will distract the mental power - that is the consciousness of the soul - thereby giving unhappiness, anxiousness, dissatisfaction, fear and so on. Instead of this if the imagination with all its emotions gets concentrated into a one-pointed imagination with some figure of imagination in the mind, then the mind becomes concentrated on that particular imagination. Just like this it happened to me on the figure of Swamiji. One positive achievement of this is that the mind becomes single-

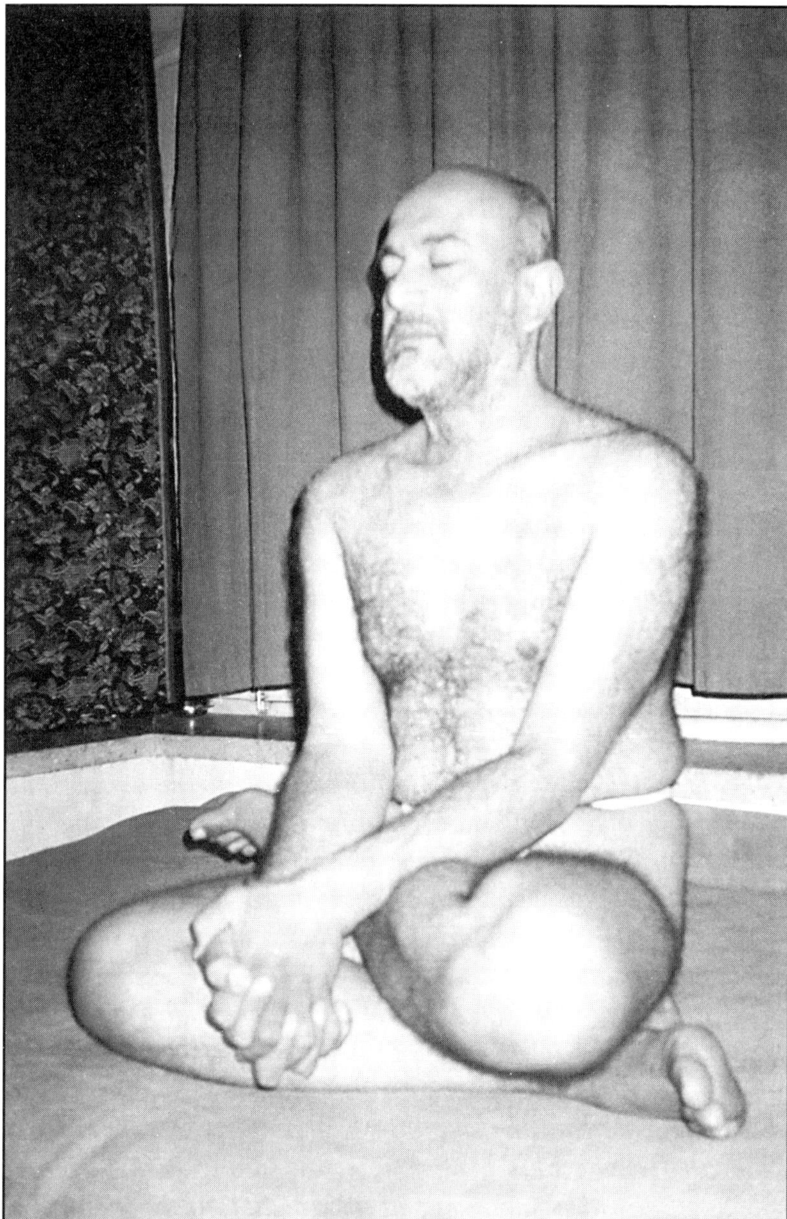

At commencement of tapas in 1994

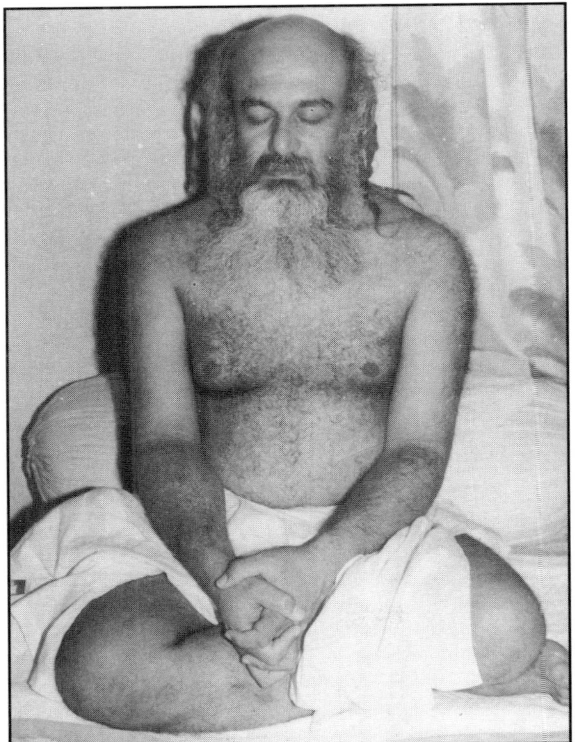

Completion of tapas in 1999

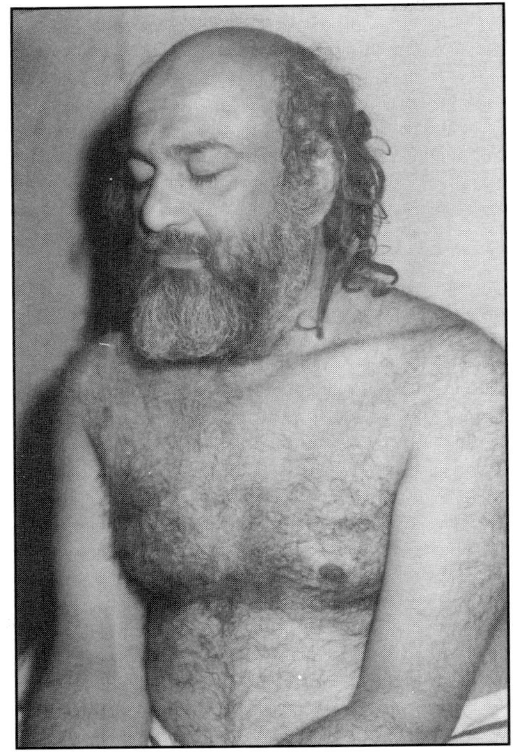

During tapas

pointed and its distractions can decrease considerably and even vanish totally. Hence the mind will not notice anything else other than that one particular imagination. Thus though it starts with a simple imagination, its single-pointedness and concentration increases tremendously by getting all the emotions tapped into a single-pointed energy.

Then in the second stage - I would call it mental projection - the mind would have achieved amazing concentration and would experience the same single imagination as a reality but still with a separate entity from itself. Thus though it actually happens from within, it would appear as if there is a scene and a separate one who sees the scene. Hence when one is capable of going into tapas, *that same scene will become a touch-bearer guide as a Guru for the mind to recede towards the real Self.*

In the third stage - when you reach the stage of tapas *- then the consciousness of that imagined self who acts as a separate seer, vanishes.*

Then a physical manifestation of that first resolution would take place. That is what we call 'God's darshan' *- a god appearing before a person. The form of that manifestation would depend on the first resolution of that mind; it can be any form of God. (Like for me, the first resolution was Swamiji and I knew Swamiji had the* darshan *of Lord Shiva and Goddess Parvati, who later merged into Him, so it happened in that way to me.) Then the same manifestation further becoming the inner guru will guide and show that everything that is watched as a separate entity from the Self is watched only by the soul's consciousness, called mind.*

So that same inner Guru which is a manifestation of the mind's resolution will also guide one to give up that resolution itself, totally, and give up the thought of 'I' - thus finally after losing all thoughts of any need, including the need of liberation, mind surrenders the thought of 'I' also.

This is only a little bit of a clue to explain, but nothing can be explained conclusively. As you progress you simply experience that the mind becomes quieter and quieter by losing all its imaginations. This somehow happens when manifestations appear and then disappear. Simply the consciousness starts gaining the awareness of its Existence. "

There was one particular vision that was re-occurring often - a vision of a train crash. In this vision He would see a lot of people - injured, dead or dying - lying around, and there was a lot of suffering. At some times he would even have the vision of his own head being cut off and lying on the ground. For a while it did disturb him. When General Haunt Singh came on one of his visits Seenu discussed it with him. The General reassured the *tapaswin* not to worry about this - he even suggested that it could have been an event from a recent previous life which might explain why this vision was recurring so very often.

When Swamiji appeared later on the full moon day of the month He also reassured the *sadhak* in the same way - that he should concentrate, that these were all simple illusions and he should not take them seriously.

He comforted His disciple, "It will all get evaporated. Just focus the attention, remain unperturbed and keep your mind with unwavering concentration between the eyebrows."

" *So thus I continued and after sometime this vision stopped occurring.*"

During the first and second years he did also feel frustration at times, but like the visions and the sounds, this frustration was really occurring as a trick of the mind - because the more the mind was getting concentrated, the more powerfully it was trying to jump back into the world.

Nonetheless, slowly the visions and mind's agitations were reducing.

So it was that after 15 months in *tapas*, with the mind still on an *asthami* day,

" *I could first feel that somebody had touched me on the forehead and gently patted to wake me up. As I opened my eyes I saw from the thin air that the manifestation of a deity was happening, surrounded by an amazing, glowing light. When it was totally completed I was in awe for a while. I was just wondering. I became dumbfounded. I couldn't think or talk - anything.*

The deity spoke very respectfully, 'May your tapas *be completed soon and you become a* Yogi *and obtain your Guru's powers and Grace.'*

It blessed me on the forehead by touching me with its fingers and uttered a mantra which sat into my mind. The deity then told me that Swamiji would come to make me to sit into the next direction, so I was just waiting for the next few days until purnami *(full moon day).*

On purnami *when Swamiji manifested with the dazzling, glowing light around Him (it was very difficult to watch continuously with the naked eyes), my total concentration was on Him. I was only conscious of Swamiji, unaware of my own body or my own existence or anything else.*

He asked me, 'What happened on the day of asthami*?'*

Then I explained to Swamiji that some other figure had awakened me and respectfully spoke, blessing me that I would become a Yogi *and obtain Guru's Grace and powers.*

Swamiji asked, 'Did you get any mantra?'

I replied, 'Yes' and repeated the mantra to Him. He directed

that in another eight days' time, on the next asthami, *I could change my direction to the East.*

He blessed me and then disappeared.

The mind was realizing its own tricks gradually. "

15

It Will All Disappear

Initially when Swamiji instructed him to change the direction from North to East, He further directed,

"You may have to do it for 1 year, 3 months. However wait until the deity comes and gives instructions. Just carry on. In the meanwhile I will come and keep blessing you. Next *purnima* I will come."

" *He appeared as He had before dropping His physical body; it was the same 'Swamiji'. He would appear from thin air and after the conversation was over, again He would disappear as I used to keep watching, amazed. This act of appearing is called 'manifestation', because after dropping His physical body, Swamiji has become one with the Divine - what we call God - which is All Pervading Spirit. The same Divine Spirit manifested always in the form of Swamiji, physically appearing and then disappearing.*

The form that I saw was of the same Swamiji with black matted hair and the face of His younger age when He used to be in His late 30's or early 40's. Also He spoke to me in Telugu, His own mother tongue. That was the way Swamiji always used to talk to me previously. His behaviour, His hands, His fingers, His way of talking - everything was the same as I knew Him during that twenty years of service before tapas *when He was physically with us. He was thus the very same Swamiji. The only difference was that He used to manifest and again disappear. When I say 'disappear' I mean He merged with the Divine again; the Divine withdrew that manifestation back into the Self. That was the only difference; otherwise, everything else was the same.*

His appearance, His behaviour, His way of teaching me lessons was very tough. He used to talk bluntly. Just like I have mentioned, even in the beginning of tapas *when He came He bluntly told me,*

'Either you have to come out as a Yogi *or your dead body will have to come out. Do not abandon the practice. Do not abandon in the middle of* tapas. *You are not going to get up and go away!'*

This was a command - a very blunt command - of what He wanted me to do. Well, this gave me a lot of energy and determination and kept me free from any fear or anxiousness.

So thus He was the same Swamiji. Only the difference was that now it was the Divine that came in the form of Swamiji - manifested in the form of Swamiji - and disappeared. I don't mean to signify that He came from somewhere - from a long distance - and that He went back to that long distance. That was not the case. After Realization He showed me these technologies, that now Swamiji is one with the Divine - both are the same.

Because the Divine is all pervading It simply manifested into that physical form for the purpose of talking because still there was some ego of 'me and the Guru' before the Nirvikalpa Samadhi[34] . *After the* Nirvikalpa Samadhi *I understood this aspect, that it was the Divine - simply a manifestation. So after the conversation was over the Divine would withdraw It's manifestation back into the Divine. That was how it used to happen.* "

Other visions still occurred and some were of a terrifying, horrifying nature. As full physical manifestations they would appear

---

[34] *Nirvikalpa Samadhi* - Nirvikalpa samadhi occurs when the mind recedes totally (called '*manolaya*' in spiritual language) and thus merges with the infinite and eternal Self.

as real as any object in this world. Some, coming in a very frightening appearance, would ferociously lunge forward as though they were going to crush his neck and kill him, making dreadful sounds and shouting, "We won't allow you to continue the *tapas*." They would try to intimidate him, shouting and threatening, "You are not born for this purpose. You cannot succeed. If you want you can go to any other world, experience any other thing, but we will not allow you to do this *tapas*."

But mostly the mind was not reacting and no fearful thoughts occurred - he just kept watching them. He observed that the manifestations vanished before actually touching him.

" *What I observed was, every time the mind remained very composed, alert and unperturbed. I could see there was total detachment -* vairagya *was there. That strong command of Swamiji was always in the mind, that either my dead body should go out or that I must become a* Yogi *and complete the* tapas *and go out. When such things used to happen, sometimes I thought, 'Even if death occurs, it is no problem.'*

Thus thinking, I used to close my eyes again and peacefully all the visions used to disappear. Nothing used to come to the mind. The mind used to go back to the stillness; it did not go into agitations.

Gradually these types of manifestations decreased but there used to be other type of troubles. Once the body fell down and the head was hit in the fall causing a swelling to develop. I did not notice this for a while, but the people who were looking after me, when they came for cleaning in the morning they observed it and told me. Gradually after they told me I started feeling the pain also. It used to be very painful. And also in the body there used to be a lot of pain. "

With the mind becoming more concentrated, its power of imagination also increased.

" *Since time immemorial and perhaps since so many lives, the mind is spread with imaginations into billions and billions of layers. When this mind is coming back to become more concentrated is the time when one gets all these visions and manifestations because the mind has resolutions with its own imaginations. Whatever it imagines the mind absorbs as an imprint and then goes on acquiring further imprints one after another, continuously.*

You wait in tapas *with all the patience so that all imaginations of the mind get wiped out. When the imprints are getting wiped out, visions and manifestations are created. Their strength of appearance and physical manifestation depends on the concentration power of the mind, just like sometimes your dreams may be very strong with a solid picturization which your mind would be unable to forget for a long time. Even after coming out of such a dream the mind would still be experiencing all the scenes of the dream like happiness, unhappiness, fear and sorrow, and so on. Sometimes the dream picturization could be quite blurred and vague in remembrance and by the time you have come out of the dream you will forget what you actually dreamed.*

As the mind recedes in tapas *and becomes more and more quiet, everything is gradually forgotten and the mind will start experiencing only the existence of its own Self.*

Total faith and determination with detachment - with these tools one will be able to see it through, otherwise it can be very maddening and one feels like banging the head and just running away like mad. I always prayed for the Guru's Grace at all such times. "

At this time even taking food became a problem - the one glass milk he would consume each day was not digestible sometimes and pimples and boils started to develop on his thighs and shoulders. He tried diluting the milk with water but when that also proved indigestible it was discontinued and he took vegetable soup, or leafy vegetables, or the whole green sprouted gram. But for a long time the pimples and boils developed on the thighs, making it difficult sometimes to sit for meditation; but he persisted and after some time they finally disappeared.

So all these types of both physical and mental troubles came often. At one time one leg mysteriously swelled up and remained that way for nearly two months, causing a great deal of pain which became almost unbearable and making it impossible to walk properly.

But he continued to sit in the meditation cycles. Swamiji had told him that he should not abandon the *sadhana* even for a single day - that was essential. Whenever Swamiji appeared He would repeatedly assure his disciple that everything would be alright and that whatever was happening was only a test of mental determination.

He always gave positive encouragement and advice.

"Whatever trouble happens, physically also, you must continue. You cannot take rest even for a day. Then that can disturb a whole month's practice of meditation. So then it may become difficult to complete the *tapas* within this five years. It may prolong for several more years if the mind loses the grip of remaining composed and being alert that everything is simply illusion, *Maya*."

In the second half of the second year he started experiencing a new type of manifested vision.

Several times on the full moon day, Swamiji manifested and he felt Him taking him by the hand and leading him off. He experienced the sensation as though he was travelling in space for a very long time and saw manifested visions of other *lokas* (distant planets). Together he and Swamiji visited these different worlds and saw various different types of creations. In one of the worlds there were only animals everywhere, while in another there were only green trees and forest and a beautifully peaceful, serene atmosphere.

" *Once I remember Swamiji had taken me to a place where*

there were a lot of people there meditating - they had a dazzling glow on their faces. They received Swamiji well and He was made to sit and they worshipped Him, offering him Pada Puja *(worshipping the feet of the Guru). I could watch all these things. And then Swamiji said, 'After your work in the world, after you complete the Mission, for some time because of your previous resolutions you will have to come to this place, live in* tapas *for some time and then after that only you will completely achieve* videhamukti *(merge totally with the Divine).*

Another time He was taking me travelling through space and all the way He was explaining the nonexistence of all the Universe, total Creation. He went on telling me, 'Creation has never happened at all. Everything that you see is your own mental resolutions. As much as the mental resolutions are true I am also here in a manifested form because of your own mental resolutions. Actually I am the Divine. Because of your mental resolutions I had to come in this form to bless and guide you.'

He went on explaining, 'Though you might see and experience different worlds, never get attracted to them. Because of your prarabdha *(previous mental resolutions) I'll be taking you to these worlds but if you get attracted then you will have to come here later, live, do* tapas *and only then become One with the Divine. If you do not get attracted, if you can totally wash your mental resolutions, then you need not have to come here. So if you can, be alert always that these things are simply illusions and do not get attracted to them - don't allow any desire to occur into your mind.*

Because of your previous resolutions I may even tell you that you will have to come and stay here for some time. Still if you can erase this thought also from your mind then you need not have to come. But if you develop any desire of coming here, then you will have to come here also after working in the world.'

So this type of guidance and advice Swamiji used to give

me constantly, to help me to remove any such desire. He used to take me to such worlds. Several places He took me, where there were people doing tapas - *all the places mostly I saw people doing* tapas.

Then I used to wonder, 'This is very amusing. I must have had the resolve to see a lot of tapas.*'*

I saw a lot of great Sages who I had heard about in the scriptures and they were sitting and doing tapas.

Then I used to think, 'Maybe these things are due to my own previous resolutions', and I used to consider that I should not get attracted to them. I would think, ' "The Divine is the Ultimate Truth" should be the Goal.' "

Swamiji repeatedly advised him, "You must be very careful. You should not allow your mind to get involved. It should not consider that such an experience is real. Ultimately this creation is unreal and is going to merge with the Supreme Divine. You must never get tempted to go into any world. If your mind gets tempted then after the *tapas* and after being in the world you will have to come to these worlds and live here and do *tapas* again, before totally merging with the Supreme Divine. So you must be very careful not to allow your mind to get attached."

" *On one occasion when Swamiji took me on such travels it appeared we had travelled for a very long time. Then it came to the mind, 'My God, now that I have been performing* tapas *and for so many years that we have been travelling, now I will have to continue again.' So then when this thought came, it occurred to me, 'It is better for me that I go back to the room and continue the* tapas - *otherwise it will remain uncompleted.'*

Then I suddenly saw Swamiji and myself entering the room and my body was sitting on the same dais. It was very amazing for me when I saw my body. As I came nearer, suddenly I felt that the body was inside me. It was a very funny, amazing experience.

Then suddenly I was in meditation and Swamiji was waking

me.

When I opened my eyes I saw Swamiji laughing, 'What happened?'

Spontaneously I replied, 'Illusion occurred.'

Then Swamiji was happy. 'If the mind is alert that everything is simply Illusion, that only the Supreme Being is the Reality, then you will be able to realize and merge with the Divine. Be firm always.'

Thus saying, Swamiji disappeared. "

Apart from the terrifying aggressive manifestations and the physical difficulties of indigestion, infections and pain, and these experiences of journeys to other *lokas* he also experienced tempting visions.

" Swamiji had told me when He manifested, 'I will come and take you around out of your body, but if any other deity, male or female, offers to take you to any other world or travelling in space, never accept such an offer. Politely refuse, saying, 'My Guru will be taking me and I would like to go with my Guru.'

Such deities did come and they tempted me so often with offers of taking me around the different creations into different worlds which they said I could conquer and live there happily while ruling over them.

Many other temptations were also given - powers.

They said, 'Whatever you resolve, within a moment that can happen. We will be at your service always to fulfill all your desires.'

But due to Swamiji's Grace the mind was firm and totally detached. I could see it never got attracted towards these offerings of all the deities. It remained composed and peaceful.

I just politely said, 'My Guru's Grace is always there. So whatever experience that one needs to have during this tapas *my Guru will show. My Guru will take me and help me.'*

Thus saying politely, I refused.

Repeatedly they offered - many times. But every time by the Grace of Swamiji, the Divine Guru Maharaj, the mind did not accept what they were offering and politely it refused.

So thus the mind was alert due to the Grace of my Guru Shivabalayogi. "

But even these were not the most severe test he experienced during this phase of the *tapas*.

Though he experienced the severe physical pain, the entrancing journeys to other *lokas*, and the temptations of powers, the most difficult test was the maddening effect which used to occur - that one should simply get up and run away. At such times he prayed to the Divine Guru to give him the ability to sit down quietly and have the mind unperturbed.

This restlessness of the mind was not just the simple vague restlessness of the normal human mind. With the mind now in such a concentrated state - concentrated to a hundred percent - its restlessness also similarly increased a million-fold. As the mind was used to being out in the world it wished to go back there and so when such a concentrated mind tried to jump back to the world, wanted to run away, then an enormous power and energy was created. Again it was the Guru's grace and his intense *vairagya* that enabled him to pass through this difficult time.

" *Mentally there used to be very maddening effects of feeling one wanted to get up and run away.*

Sometimes one used to feel, 'Now it is really not possible to sit down, to remain peacefully.' I think the mind was trying to come out with all its force.

At that time the potency of concentration had increased enormously. Previously the mind has been spread out into the universe in billions of pieces, so when it was brought back and concentrated into one piece, the risk factor of it jumping back into the universe increases tremendously at that time. You can imagine just as when gas is compressed into a cylinder, if it bursts open how powerful it will be - it will be like a bomb blast. In the same way it used to appear sometimes that now my head was going to burst open. There used to be very heavy pain all about the head and neck. I used to feel now that if I do not get up my head may burst into pieces. There was also a lot of burning sensation along the back, feeling like a fire burning inside the body.

But finally the Guru's Grace and blessings enabled me to keep going."

Initially when Swamiji directed him to change the direction from North to East He told his disciple that the *tapas* would need to be performed facing East for at least the same period as when he had faced North - for one year three months - but to wait until the deity came, blessed him and gave instructions on changing direction.

At the end of this period, on the *ashtami*[35] day, after one year and three months facing the East he again experienced the sensation of being patted on the head and slowly came out of meditation. As he watched he saw the inexplicable, amazing, glowing form of the deity manifest standing in front of him.

However this time the deity did not speak but simply stood in front of him for a while, smilingly silently and then disappeared. As no mantra came and the deity did not speak, he was unsure of what he should do but decided to continue on facing the same eastern direction.

A few days later on *purnima* when Swamiji appeared He asked His disciple what had occurred. Hearing the recounted story of what had transpired, he asked the *tapaswin*,

"Didn't the Deity tell you any mantra or did not He speak to you?"

On hearing that no mantra was given and that the deity did not speak at all, Swamiji informed him that this meant that he

[35] *Ashtami* - The eighth day of the Indian Lunar fortnight (i.e. eighth day after new moon or full moon).

would have to keep sitting facing the East for at least a further six months but that at the end of this extended period the deity would probably come again and then give the mantra.

"And that means you will have more a troubling period in this next six months. You must look after your mind so that it does not get either disturbed or involved in the manifested visions or any experiences that occur. You must be very alert that 'Everything is only mentally resoluted illusions.' "

Saying this Swamiji then disappeared and the *tapas* in the easterly direction continued for another six months.

" *So thus my* tapas *facing towards the East direction prolonged to one year, nine months - up to 10th November, 1997 which was again an* ashtami.

The deity blessed me as the first deity had done, speaking very respectfully in a reverent way, 'May your tapas *be completed and may you become a* Yogi *and obtain Guru's Grace and powers.'*

After that, the deity uttered the mantra for the westerly direction and then disappeared.

Eight days later, on the next purnima, when Swamiji came and asked me what had taken place, I told Him that this time the mantra had come.

He replied, 'Now you can change your direction to the West. Your experiences when facing towards the East have been more troublesome - bodily and also mentally. So now that's why you will be able to complete the West direction easily[36]*. If you can steadily continue, do it for the next eight months or one year. Let me see how much the mind can remain composed in its agitation.'*

---

[36] *Tapas in the four cardinal directions*: As the mind is under the influence of two main illusions - space and time - the *tapas* performed in the four compass directions overcomes the effects of the relatively of space on the mind.

16

Realization

In the later part of the time spent facing the East the mind had learnt to remain quiet - not to get agitated, worried, inquisitive or curious. It had learnt not to analyze or make judgments. All these activities of the mind had stopped, though visions and total physical manifestations were still occurring.

" *By the third year I saw the mind becoming totally quiet - 'standstillness' had occurred. But because its acquired habits were not completely erased, because it had not yet become totally purified, that was why all the manifestations and visions were still happening. But the mind was not getting perturbed anymore. It quietly watched.*

It was ready to die as the mind had become totally alert that the ' Self is Spirit ' and ' I am not this body '. So that attachment to the body consciousness was totally gone and an awareness came that even if this body goes, nothing will happen to me. This alertness was there so I was never bothered by visions or manifestations. "

By the last two or three months of the period of *tapas* facing the East, all the visions and manifestations finally disappeared, so that the mind became totally composed. Hence this period passed very quickly for him - the passage of time was barely noticeable. Gradually he had become totally unaware of the body or surroundings and he felt no pain when in this state - only when he came out of this mind-stilled state and regained bodily consciousness would he become aware of the enormous pain in his body. However though unaware of his body and surroundings, that supreme consciousness of Existence was always present.

Subsequently when the period facing the West commenced the mind was already quiet -it was by now becoming more purified as the acquired habits were being wiped away completely. So gradually the state of *samadhi* was occurring.

" *After the third year was over* samadhi *was occurring - the mind had become totally thoughtless.*

It had stopped getting agitated. It had stopped taking any further imprints into itself.

Gradually I had started experiencing simply the awareness of the Self. I was totally conscious of my Existence, totally aware of my Existence and there was no definition of thought in the mind that ' I ' am. That also had vanished and there was no awareness of body in that consciousness, no awareness of any surroundings even when I used to open the eyes for a while.

Also whatever vision I saw - this world or people coming, going, doing prostrations... watching for some time... and the body and the food, people who were serving me... it all appeared very vague and nothing really appeared serious or real for me. It appeared as if I was dreaming for a while and that dream was over the moment I used to close the eyes. No vision used to come to the mind. So I think this was how the samadhi *came to me.* "

In the third and fourth years of *tapas* Swamiji instructed him to start giving *darshan* to devotees who came. They were allowed to visit during the nighttime and would simply come and sit in the *tapaswin's* presence. Later, regular *darshan* sessions were started on Sundays at which a few devotees would come and also sit for meditation. At times they would ask questions and though he by habit usually remained in silence, still he was able to answer their queries spontaneously when the questions were put to him -

the answers would automatically come without a thought process. He noted that the mind had stopped taking imprints from these experiences. If devotees came with queries about difficulties they were experiencing in their lives, he would pray to the Divine Guru to help them and then found that the mind became peaceful again spontaneously - it was not getting involved, developing attachments or taking imprints.

He lost the experience of any past or future and was simply aware of Existence. Also sometimes when he did return to a bodily awareness he was now aware of his body as though it was inside him, rather than feeling that he was inside the body.

Swamiji's manifestation still occurred on the full moon days and in the fourth year on one of these sacred occasions, his Divine Guru blessed him with a new name -"Shivarudra Balayogi". "*Shiva*" " indicating the state of complete stand-stillness of the mind," "*Rudra* " signifying that immense creative energy released at the time of creation, " *Bala* " meaning a young boy - the attitude of a dear son he had always adopted with his Guru and is also one of the names of Lord Shiva's consort, Parvati, and " *Yogi* " denoting one who has attained the state of ' Yoga ' - union with the Divine Self.

Finally in November 1998 on the *ashtami* day the deity for the West manifested, blessed him reverentially as those previously had done and gave the mantra for the next direction. When Swamiji appeared on the next *purnima* the *tapaswin* described the manifestation to his Divine Guru who instructed him to turn to the South for eight months for the next phase of the *tapas.*

Entering the final year of his *tapas* the mind had settled completely and was in *samadhi*, though a faint awareness of the existence of " I " still remained. This had to disappear and the need for Realization itself also had to vanish, so simply all that could be done was to wait - effort ceased. He had simply to wait thus, patiently, quietly concentrating, without trying to resolve anything mentally.

" *For the next eight months it went very peacefully. The experience that the awareness has, is the Supreme Bliss. You would have never experienced anything of this creation, in the universe, ever - from any material thing that is available - such as the Supreme Bliss that you experience in this state. But one needs to be very careful to have total contentment,* vairagya *(detachment) and patience.* "

In this blissful stage the danger occurs that the *sadhak's* mind may become excited by the experience. For it is an experience within the creation – a 'higher level' of experience, but still outside the Self. Thus the mind can start getting involved in the experience and start developing thoughts and imaginations again. While in this bliss the mind is likely to start thinking, 'Oh I'm getting closer and will become Realized soon.'

When this blissfulness occurs, when the mind becomes excited, it is likely to try to jump back to this world, to this creation. Also some *siddhis*[37] might come – the mind at this stage becomes so concentrated that if one resolve something in the mind, then that thing can simply happen straight away. Thus one might feel more excited that some powers have come, then greed may come and the mind might jump back into the world. So the directive given is that one has to patiently wait through this stage with total detachment to all of the creation. With all the experiences - except for that of the Self - one must wait, totally surrendered until the mind totally recedes and merges with the Self and effortlessly, peacefully remains there, totally contented in that Supreme Peace.

---

[37] 'Powers' , *lit.* 'Perfections' – At the stage where the mind has become totally concentrated, its inherent capacity to 'Imagine' reaches its highest pitch, such that whatever you resolve in the mind will occur in the creation instantly. See Glossary.

" *Many* sadhaks *tend to think the* tapas *is over when this type of Supreme Bliss stage comes - but one has to wait until the Absolute Peace is achieved, meaning the mind has to totally recede and become one with the Self and remain thus effortlessly with contentment.*

During this period nothing occurs to the mind, even the thought of ' I ', existence of ' I ', the need for liberation, the need for samadhi, *Self Realization, or God – nothing occurs to the mind. All your prayers also come to an end. It does not occur to the mind to pray anything because there is nothing. So you gain simply the consciousness of Existence. You become aware of your Existence but you do not think that ' I exist ' or this is ' I '. You simply lose the thought of ' I ' also.*

But there is one thing which can happen during this period. One can go into yoga nidra. Yoga nidra *means, when you are in a deep state of* samadhi *you are likely to become totally unconscious for long periods. My elderly* Gurubhai *(brother disciple) who I honor very much, General Hanut Singh, once came to talk to me during this period and I told him about this. Quoting Maharshi Ramana and Swamiji's advice he advised me that I must take care not to lose total consciousness. I must not become unconscious. That is called* yoga nidra *and further progress of the mind would get curtailed. That should not happen. So he advised me that I must maintain my consciousness of Existence so that the* tapas *may continue towards its culmination. So I prayed to the Divine Guru to help me to maintain this consciousness of Existence.*

Gradually my tapas *progressed peacefully. I always had the awareness of Existence. Thus in* samadhi *also one must remember that you do not vanish. Your Existence is always there. Only the thought of ' I, mine, me, God ', every thing vanishes. To say in other words, there is no seen or seer because you alone exist. The consciousness of Existence, Awareness always is there. Thus you progress towards the* Nirvikalpa Samadhi. "

The *tapas* facing the South was completed on 10th July, 1999 when the deity appeared, blessed him respectfully, "May you become a *Yogi* and obtain the Guru's Grace and powers", and bestowed the mantra for the next direction - an invocation to Lord Shiva, the supreme Guru.

A few days later on the next *purnima* which was the auspicious day of *Guru Purnima*[38], Swamiji again manifested and told him that he could change direction to face the North, facing towards Mount Kailas (Lord Shiva's adobe) to invoke Lord Shiva's appearance, as *Paramaguru* (the Guru's Guru).

" *Our* Guru Parampara *(lineage of Gurus) starts from Lord Shiva so Swamiji, the Divine Guru, advised me to invoke the darshan of Lord Shiva. Thus I started* tapas *facing North on the Guru Purnima day in July, 1999.*"

Throughout the five years various groups of people had tried to distract his *tapas*, but he remained composed, forgiving them all - for he saw all with an equal eye, witnessing the Self everywhere. These tests came to a climax towards the end of his *tapas*. In one incident a lady from south India came to the ashram saying she wished to have his *darshan*, but unfortunately as she had come during the day and at that time the *tapaswin* was only giving *darshan* in the night hours. The doors to the room were locked and so the ashram staff told her, "We're sorry it's not possible to open the doors at this time." She waited a few more hours and then left, but she later began to claim she was an incarnation of Goddess and tried to misuse Sri Shivarudra Balayogi's name, saying that during her Dehra Dun visit she had entered his *tapas* room in an infinite astral form and had blessed Him, and that it was he who had first declared her to be an incarnation of Goddess. This of

[38] *Guru Purnima* - The full moon on the Indian calendar dedicated to Guru, when all the disciples offer their respects, honour and surrender to the Lotus Feet of the Guru.

course was just a made-up story, a gimmick to attempt to increase her status, as no such thing had ever occurred.

He always considered such elements as God's tests for determination and purity of heart and never wanted to compromise on the aim of total Self-Realization. He prayed to the Guru that the mind should lose all imaginations including the thoughts of " I ", or the need of " mine " and also the need for liberation.

The last test from the creation was a deep one. His mother, Sharada, had fallen ill when he was in the middle of the *tapas* but, to avoid disturbing him in any way, had made sure that no one in the family directly or indirectly allowed him to become aware of it. Her selfless wish was for him to complete the *tapas* successfully and emerge Self-Realized. However finally in this last period of his *tapas* she felt that her physical body would not be able to endure much longer on this Earth and so wanting to have his *darshan* before leaving this world, she requested that the family organize for her to travel to Dehra Dun. Though quite ill she undertook the long and arduous journey from her home in Bangalore to Dehra Dun by train and car.

She was overjoyed to behold her dear youngest son as a *Yogi* in *tapas*, and although in those days he was in deep *dhyana* for the whole day he would allow people to have *darshan* in the night around 10 o'clock. At these times he would usually remain silent with eyes closed or half-closed but when his mother came for *darshan* he spoke with her and enquired about her health. She stayed for only four days as she did not want to disturb his *tapas*, saying, "I am grateful to God and Guru Maharaj that I got a chance to have your *darshan*. If I stay for more days you might get disturbed, so better I leave."

She departed this world on 8th October 1999, in the final months of his *tapas*. He had been instructed by Swamiji not to leave the room and thus was unable to attend to any of the rites for her funeral.

" *Even for* Yogis *a mother is very special. The great saint*

Adi Shankara went to see His mother as promised from the midst of His spiritual tours. Sri Ramana Maharshi sat with His mother on her last day to liberate her from the bondage of the cycle of birth and death.

This was another test for me. "

For four months Shivarudra Balayogi sat facing Mount Kailas in the North. As Swamiji considered Lord Shiva as His Guru, He had instructed His disciple that it was proper that he seek Lord Shiva's blessing for the completion of *tapas*. This period went very peacefully. The mind had become totally peaceful and the *Balayogi* was experiencing consciousness of Existence - the thought of " I " had totally vanished and the need for *samadhi* had disappeared. There was simply Awareness.

Visions and manifestations (other than the manifestation of Swamiji on *purnima*) had now ceased, except for one vision which came during this period facing Mount Kailas.

In this, he saw Swamiji praying to Lord Shiva to bless His disciple to complete the *tapas* successfully. To this request Lord Shiva smilingly replied,

"Nothing can be given without tests. Anyone will get it only on eligibility."

Then in the vision Swamiji blessed his disciple that he might remain composed and unperturbed, whatever may come.

On the *purnima* days Swamiji still came and gave *darshan* and continued to inspire him to carry on, "Be composed and nothing will happen. Everything will be alright. Just do not succumb to any disturbances."

In October during the full moon day *darshan* when Swamiji came He assured His disciple that this *samadhi* was total and final and directed him, "You can come out formally on the next full moon day." During this visit his Guru let him know there would be one final test, though He did not say what it would entail. Hearing that the *tapas* was now nearly complete and that he could formally come out in one month's time, Sri Shivarudra Balayogi informed the devotees who were attending to him that he would be able to come out of his tapas on the next *purnima - Kartik Purnima* in the Indian calendar - and would give *darshan* to all who came. They prayed that they would like to organize a function, informing all the devotees and inviting them to come and have *darshan* on that auspicious day, to which he assented.

On the next *ashtami* day on the day of *Kartik Shuklapaksham*, 16th November, he was summoned from *samadhi* by the wondrous manifestation of the deity Ardhanarishwara - half the body was Lord Shiva and half was Goddess Parvati. He slowly came out of the deep *samadhi* and took some time to realize that the manifestation had occurred.

Enraptured, he prostrated and They blessed him, telling him his *tapas* was now complete,

" Now that We have come due to your *tapas*, you do not require your Guru and can go ahead to get many followers."

But this was the crucial final test to see if any remnant ego remained; if the total surrender of the mind into the Self had taken place.

" *As no such worldly desires remained in any form or in consciousness, spontaneously I said, 'I want only the Lotus Feet of my Guru. I offer my life at the Lotus Feet of the Divine Guru who helped and guided me to this. So please, if you want to bless me, bless me that I can always remain at the Lotus Feet of my Guru and serve Him and work according to my Guru's guidance.*

It is the Guru's Grace which is needed and nothing else. Whatever the Guru my beloved Swamiji wants I will do and there is no other desire. "

Pleased with this reply, with a smile the divine

Ardhanarishwara blessed the *Yogi* that the Guru's Grace would descend and he would be able to work according to the Guru's instructions and guidance and then the deity disappeared.

Sri Shivarudra Balayogi observed that the manifestation had come out of the Self and finally merged back into It.

Then, as the form of Ardhanarishwara vanished, he witnessed his beloved Divine Guru Shivabalayogi materializing in the same place where Ardhanarishwara had been standing.

" *It occurred to me, 'This Ardhanarishwara is none other than my Divine Guru Swamiji and my Divine Guru Swamiji is none other than Ardhanarishwara, the Divine* Paramatma.'

Swamiji asked me what happened and I told him what had occurred.

He told me, 'So after you come out of the tapas, *inspire the people of this world to practice this* dhyana *meditation and know themselves. Through this practice they can achieve total peace.'*

I prayed to Swamiji to be with me always, to guide, bless and inspire me. "

Thus with all the mind's imaginations cleared, the mind in standstillness, settled now into the Self and remaining there permanently, that state was attained which is described in the Guru Gita :-

" Brahmanandam Paramasukadam
Kevalam Jnanamurtim
Dvandvaateetam Gaganasadrisham
Tattvamasyadi Lakshiyam
Ekam Nityam Vimalam Achalam

Sarvadhi Sakshi Bhutam
Bhava Teetam Triguna Rahitam
Sadgurum Tvam Namami "

" That enjoyer of the bliss of Brahman, beyond all imaginations, in supreme happiness, that personification of ultimate knowledge, having risen above the dualities of the creation, all pervasive and pure supreme consciousness, whose attention is always on That which is beyond the creation, existing as a single all-pervading entity, immortal, composed and at peace in itself, unmoved, and only a witness to everything, beyond all emotions, above the three creative qualities of the universe – to that Sadguru[39] I prostrate. "

Beyond description, defying definition, that state is beyond the ability of the mind to understand.

He Himself put it simply,

" ***Finally there remained an Awareness of a Supremely Peaceful Existence.*** "

---

[39] Sadguru - also Satguru - ' Sad / Sat ' meaning Truth, ' Guru ' - thus ' Guru of the Truth'. See Glossary.

Baba in 2005 re-visiting Naagara Teertha cave where he practiced sadhana as teenager

Baba Sri Shivarudra Balayogi Maharaj

17

The Mission Continues

The devotees at the ashram, having been told that He was due to come out on 23rd November, organized a nine day recitation of the epic Ramayana and a Laghu Rudra Homam (five day fire ceremony) with both culminating on that propitious day.

Finally on that *Kartik Purnima*, 23rd November 1999, after five years of *tapas* sitting in the room in the ashram, Baba Sri Shivarudra Balayogi Maharaj emerged into the world accompanied by the Vedic chants of the priests, and the prayers and adoration of the devotees.

Baba went first to the *Dhyana Mandir* (meditation hall) and offered worship to Sri Sri Sri Shivabalayogi's *gaddi* (dais). From there He came downstairs to offer worship to the Shivalingam and also offered *purnavati* (final offering) to mark the completion of the *homam*.

Then Baba was lead onto a dais from which He gave *darshan* to the congregation, accompanied by the singing of *bhajans* by devotees. He addressed the gathering, conveying the message that human birth is a rare gem and this life should be utilized to realize the Self, as we are that Immortal Soul beyond this physical body. The ashram trustees and devotees had organized a free medical camp and mass feeding for all the poor and needy of the area - more than 2000 people were present.

For one year Baba remained in Dehra Dun and did not go anywhere. Then in December 2000 He left Dehra Dun accompanied by some devotees and visited Adivarapupeta - where His beloved Guru Swamiji was born, performed *tapas* and attained *Mahasamadhi.* Here He paid *shradhanjali* (tribute) to the *Mahasamadhi* of His beloved Guru and was received by the trustees of the ashram there with all the due honours.

Addressing the assembled congregation Baba conveyed the message,

" *I have not come to take my Guru's place, but to serve the devotees by remaining at the Lotus Feet of beloved Guru Swamiji.*"

He told the assembled devotees that nobody can take a Guru's place and that Swamiji is all-pervading Divine; all those who really loved Swamiji would find their beloved Swamiji within their Self.

" *All one has to do is withdraw the mind and make it go introverted towards the Self. This is possible with a real* sadhana *of meditation by total faith, devotion and surrender.* "

Later He also visited Swamiji's Bangalore Ashram and toured in and around Bangalore giving *darshan* to devotees. With a group of devotees Baba also went to the pilgrimage centres of Tiruputi and Puri Jaganath.

In 2001 some devotees invited Baba to visit Singapore and Malaysia, and so in May 2001 He embarked on His first overseas tour to these countries. During the time of His *tapas* a dedicated group of devotees in America who had met Swamiji became devoted to Baba, attracted by His genuine teachings of meditation and devotion. Looking at Baba as a worthy disciple of the beloved Guru Shivabalayogi, they wanted Baba to visit America to continue Swamiji's teachings for genuine spiritual seekers.

In the meanwhile a small group of devotees from Australia were visiting the Adivarapupeta and Bangalore Ashrams and,

Baba in old age home Blessing a Devotee

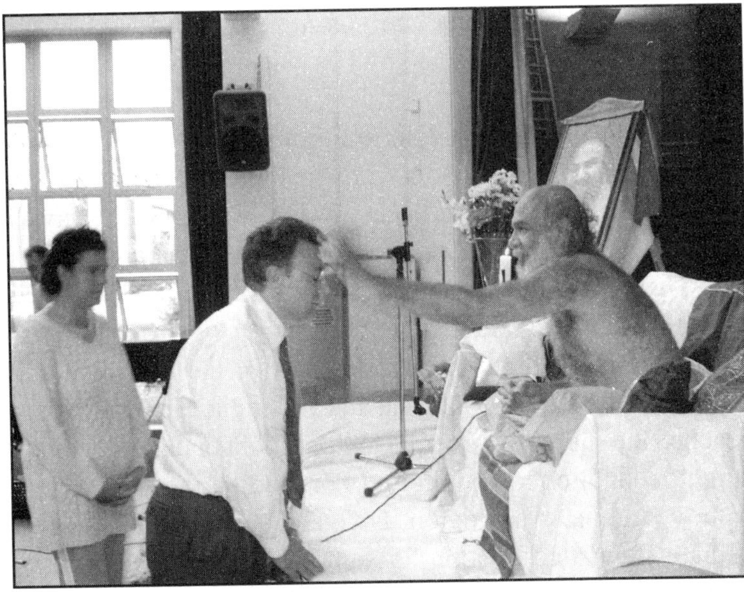

Baba initiating a Devotee

Baba giving message to devotees

coming to know about Baba and His *tapas*, visited Him in the Dehra Dun ashram and attracted by His teachings, invited Him to visit Perth.

Thus He paid His first visit to Perth in October 2001 when He toured Singapore, Malaysia, Bali in Indonesia and Perth in Australia. Since then He has been visiting Singapore, Malaysia and Perth regularly twice a year, continuing the teaching of His beloved Guru Swamiji - meditation for mind control, devotion and surrender with total faith.

In 2004 He undertook a world tour for the first time and after a visit to Singapore, Malaysia and Australia, He travelled on and reached the shores of America to the delight of devotees there. He taught meditation in and around Portland on the West Coast, Colorado, Virginia, Washington, D.C. and several other venues. From there He visited London for some days before returning to the Dehra Dun ashram.

Baba describes the aim of all spiritual pursuits simply, yet with absolute completeness. He teaches that the mind has come out of the Self, and so it is through that mind itself that one can again contact the Self. The mind is only ever searching for happiness but can never find it permanently in the creation, as the creation itself is always changing - nothing in it is permanent. He conveys the real *sadhana,* directing that in any true spiritual exercise you undertake, when God and Guru's Grace also descends, then the mind must recede and go introverted towards the Self - such a *sadhana* is genuine and worthwhile.

" *You have forgotten your real Self. You are that Abode of Supreme Peace.*

You have to experience the Truth. No matter how many lectures you listen to or scriptures you read, your own experience will make a lot of difference.

The Guru and Divine are within your Self."

Thus the Mission continues with Baba spreading the message and name of His Beloved Divine Guru, Sri Sri Sri Shivabalayogi Maharaj.

Glossary

Abhishekam - An Indian tradition of ceremonial worship by pouring liquids over an idol, symbolizing the unbroken flow of consciousness towards the Divine which occurs in meditation.

Adi Shankaracharya - 'First Shankaracharya' - Great Yogi-philosopher who expounded '*Advaita*' (Non-Dualism) which describes the Ultimate Reality as only One. He composed many famous songs variously depicting this non-dual philosophy, but also many songs of great devotion to God in a variety of forms such as Shiva, Goddess and others. He established four main monasteries at the four corners of India and those saints who headed the monasteries over the centuries have also born the title 'Shankaracharya'.

Arathi - A ceremonial salute with light performed to sacred objects such as sacred idols or the physical form or picture of the Guru.

Ashtami - The eighth day of the Indian Lunar fortnight (i.e. eighth day after new moon or full moon).

Baba, Babaji - 'Baba' meaning 'father', and the suffix 'ji' is added in India to denote an additional level of respect. Short affectionate term used in referring to Sri Shivarudra Balayogi Maharaj.

Brahmin - also *Brahman* - Indian society was organized into castes reflecting the different functions necessary in any society, including for instance agriculture, commerce, governance and religious duties. Traditionally the duty of those born in the *Brahmin* caste was to carry on the religious studies and observances of the society.

Darshan - *Darshan* is a precious spiritual exercise for the devotee's eyes. To meet a *Yogi* is also *darshan*. At such special times of seeing a *Yogi*, the individual soul's consciousness would receive the positive vibrations and absorb subtle impressions. This is always beneficial for the soul's spiritual journey.

Dhyana - lit 'Attention to'. The technique of meditation into which Swamiji was initiated by Lord Shiva and into which He in turn initiated aspirants who came to Him. Babaji carries on this mission in Swamiji's name.

Guru - lit 'Dispeller of Darkness'. One who guides the aspirant to Self-Realization. There is no English word which adequately depicts the concept, but it might be seen as a mixture of teacher / guide / protector.

Hanuman - Lord Sri Rama's great devotee, extolled throughout India as a perfect disciple.

Homam - A Hindu rite of fire sacrifice in which ghee, grains and other particular items are offered into a sanctified fire accompanied by the recitation of *mantras* (sacred words). This is symbolic of offering the thoughts of the mind into the sacred, all-consuming fire of Divine Knowledge.

Pada Puja - An Indian tradition of worshipping the Guru's feet as the most sacred object in this world.

Prasadam - Food which has been blessed by a Yogi or ceremonially offered to God before being consumed. *Prasadam* carries a spiritual vibration which elevates those who partake of it.

Puja - Ceremonial worship involving such elements as the recitation of *mantras* (sacred words), *abhishekam*, offering of flowers, *prasadam* and other items, symbolizing offering purified thoughts and consciousness to the Divine.

Purnima (also Purnami) - Full moon day.

Rama - Great Self-Realized king of ancient India whose legendary story is depicted in the epic 'Ramayana'. In the epic tale, his wife Sita is kidnapped by the demon-king Ravana but Rama rescues her. This depicts the 'kidnapping' of the mind by the illusion of the world, taking it away from its true home in the Self.

Rishi - Sage

Sadguru - also Satguru - ' Sad / Sat ' meaning Truth, ' Guru ' - thus 'Guru of the Truth' ; 'True Guru'.

Sadhak - One who practices *sadhana* (spiritual exercises); aspirant.

Sadhana - The spiritual aspirant's exercises and efforts to attain Self-Realization.

Samadhi - Standstillness of the mind. A state in which the mind experiences no thoughts, but simply Awareness, being withdrawn into the Self. Nirvikalpa samadhi occurs when the mind recedes totally (called '*manolaya*' in spiritual language) and thus merges with the infinite and eternal Self.

Sannyas - Ancient Indian order of monkhood.

Sannyasi (also Sannyasin) - Monk

Shankaracharya - see 'Adi Shankaracharya'.

Shiva - Shiva is one of the Trinities of the concept of God in Hinduism. Baba further explains, *"Shiva means the Self's existence in the total thoughtlessness state of Mahasamadhi. Shiva's concept is also the withdrawal of the illusory creation back into the Self."*

Shivabalayogi - Swamiji was initially named 'Shivabala Yogeshwara' by Lord Shiva - "Shiva" is the supreme Lord ; "Bala" is another name for Parvati, Lord Shiva's consort; "Yogeshwara" means 'Lord of Yogis'. He later changed His name to 'Shivabalayogi' to reduce confusion. "Shiva" refers to Lord Shiva, the supreme Lord; "Bala" means a small boy, but is also one of the names of Lord Shiva's consort, Parvati; "Yogi" means one who has become one with the Self. Thus the name can be read two ways - either "the Yogi devoted to Shiva and Bala" or "the boy Yogi devoted to Lord Shiva".
The title "Maharaj" (great king) is often added as a way of denoting, in Indian tradition, the great respect in which He is held.

Shivalingam - A symbolic representation of Lord Shiva, portrayed as an elliptical stone icon and used for ceremonial worship.

Siddhis - 'Powers' - At the stage in *tapas* where the mind has become totally concentrated, its inherent capacity to 'Imagine' reaches its highest

pitch, such that whatever one resolves in the mind will occur in the creation instantly.
The Indian scriptures have always warned of the dangers of this in distracting the *sadhak* from the true goal of spiritual practices which is not to attain 'powers', but to merge the mind again into the Self.

Sri - 'Blessed' . A title used in India to denote a sacred personality, a saint.

Swamiji - 'Swami' meaning 'monk', member of the Swami order, that ancient Indian order of monkhood. The suffix 'ji' is added in India to denote an additional level of respect. In this book, 'Swamiji' is particularly used to refer to Baba's *guru*, Sri Sri Sri Shivabalayogi Maharaj.

Tapas - Spiritual practice of meditation for extended periods of at least 7 to 8 hours at a time carried out continually over several years.
" *If you try to hold the mind still, focused on one point for only a minute or two - for only a moment or two - you will find how difficult it is. However if one can focus the mind like this, single-pointedly focused on one point without any thoughts for one whole hour, then one is said to be meditating. If one can meditate like this for seven to eight hours at a stretch, then one is said to be performing* tapas. "

Tapas Purthi - Celebration of a *Yogi's tapas* anniversary. In the case of both Swamiji and Baba they commenced and also emerged from their *tapas* on the same calendar day - Swamiji performed *tapas* from 7th August 1949 to 7th August 1961, and Baba 10th November 1994 to 10th November 1999.

Tapaswin - One who is engaged in *tapas*.

Vibhuti - A mixture of herbs and ash commonly used in ceremonial worship in India and used by Swamiji and Baba as a physical vehicle to transmit their blessings to devotees.

Yoga - from the Sanskrit root - 'to Unite' - The spiritual path which seeks to unite the mind with its ultimate source, the real Self.

Yogi - One who has fulfilled the path of Yoga and become one with the Divine Consciousness.

More Information

is available on the website - www.shivarudrabalayogi.com or send e-mail to cah@gorge.net.
For spiritual questions to Baba, please use the email address srby@gorge.net.

INDIA
SHIVABALAYOGI MAHARAJ TRUST
180-C, RAJPUR ROAD, RAJPUR P.O.,
DEHRA DUN - 248009 (UTTARANCHAL)

U.S.A.
Charles & Carol Hopkins
241 Cooper Avenue
Underwood, WA 98651
Phone : 509-493-5209
E-mail : cah@gorge.net

Stephen Scheer
14956 NW Mill Road
Portland, OR 97231
Phone : 503-285-6756
E-mail : scc17@aol.com

AUSTRALIA
Doris Brophy
25 Truslove Way
Duncraig, W.A. 6023.
Phone: Australia (08) 9447-2126
Email : dorisb@iinet.net.au

Anu Young
3 Hermite Rise
Sorrento, W.A. 6020
Phone: Australia(08)9448-8589
Email : anuyoung@hotmail.com

ENGLAND
Email : Shivarudra_uk@yahoo.co.uk

SINGAPORE
Mr Vijay
Block. 657, Hougang,
Avenue. 8, # 09 - 433.
Singapore. 530657
Phone : Singapore 63868044
Email: vjk999@singnet.com.sg